CORRELATIONS®
Celebrity

WILLIAM ROGERS

iUniverse, Inc.
Bloomington

Celebrity - Easy

iUniverse books may be ordered through booksellers or by contacting:

iUniverse
1663 Liberty Drive
Bloomington, IN 47403
www.iuniverse.com
1-800-Authors (1-800-288-4677)

ISBN: 978-1-4759-8495-8 (sc)
ISBN: 978-1-4759-8496-5 (ebk)

Printed in the United States of America

iUniverse rev. date: 04/04/2013

CORRELATIONS

Dear Consumer,

     Congratulations! You have just purchased a one of a kind puzzle that is geared towards education while also having fun. I have worked diligently to create a style of puzzle that is different from the rest and that would stand out easily above all the others. <u>Correlations</u> is a puzzle that is educational and equipped to enhance the minds of others. This style of puzzle originated out of the thought of making math fun. I wanted to create a puzzle that would help people learn or re-learn the basic math concepts and create different levels in which people could try to conquer. <u>Correlations</u> is suitable for all ages of people whether young or old. This puzzle can be formatted for those who want to take it easy and for those who like a little challenge.

     <u>Correlations</u> is like an enhanced mathematical word search. I have enjoyed bringing this new style of puzzle to the market, and I hope you enjoy doing this puzzle as much as I have enjoyed creating it. Nothing is too hard to do if you just set your mind to it. <u>Correlations</u> is going to challenge you when it comes to math and searching for the words within the puzzle. Congratulations once again, and I hope you have a blast on your <u>Correlations</u> journey!

William S. Rogers III

How to Solve Correlations

- The puzzles consist of a 7x7 grid
- Solve the math within the box and try to figure out what letters go where
- You do this by knowing where each letter falls in the alphabet (EX: A=1, K=11, P=16, T=20)
- EX: To find the letter B you would look for 1+1. This comes out to equal 2=B
- Once you figure this out you have to find the words within the puzzle
- EX: GREEK – the words are not all straight or diagonal. As long as the G is touching the R box, the R is touching the E box, the E is touching the E box, and the E is touching the K box then the word is found within the puzzle
- The letters within the puzzles are only used once (**NO ONE LETTER OR BOX CAN BE USED TWICE**)
- All the boxes within the puzzle are not to be filled
- (1) (2) (3) (4) – These are used to identify the words on the Answer Sheets

Take this 7 X 7-square example on this page

12+3	4+5	16+3	14+4	6+5	7+2	2+0=B (4)
3+4	2+2=D (2)	10+4=N (2)	4+1	22+3=Y (4)	1+0=A (4)	8+6
9+10	1+0=A (2)	3+3	1+2=C (2)	2+3=E (2)	14+4=R (4)	9+2=K (4)
15+5	12+2	11+6	10+5=O (1)	7+1	4+1=E (4)	16+5
14+4	11+4=O (3)	4+5=I (1)	4+1=E (3)	6+7=M (1)	5+6	17+5
12+12=X (3)	1+8	1+1=B (3)	11+8=S (1)	5+6=K (3)	13+8=U (3)	9+2
5+5	6+12	1+4	5+2	12+8=T (1)	3+4	5+5=J (3)

<u>WORDS</u>

1. MOIST (13, 15, 9, 19, 20)
2. DANCE (4, 1, 14, 3, 5)
3. JUKEBOX (10, 21, 11, 5, 2, 15, 24)
4. BAKERY (2, 1, 11, 5, 18, 25)

To start, look for a word that have letters that are not in the other words. The word JUKEBOX; locate the J first by finding 2 numbers that add up to 10. Starting off there are 2 boxes in this puzzle with the sum of 10; in the lower left hand corner and in the lower right hand corner. The one in the right hand corner is the only one that has the letter U connected to it with 13+8. After this there are 3 boxes which contains multiples that equal K; 9+2 to the right, 5+6 up above, and 5+6 to the left. When a situation like this arises in a puzzle, the best thing to do is to plan ahead and look for

'ay you should go. So

above and the

liscover that the

efore, the K

that K is

box in

om that box.

onal from each other.

the puzzle. All the

e word to be found within the

id the word JUKEBOX, plan ahead

in the word you are trying to find.

JX is found use the Elimination Process

not being able to reuse those same boxes over

er problem arises like this one.

liscovers that a word is too hard to find, locate part of the
rd within the puzzle first, stop, and search for a new word. This
often helps because searching for a new word can eliminate some
of the boxes that you may have thought were going to be used for
the first word you were searching for. There is no guess work that
needs to be done when it comes to these puzzles. All you have to
do is solve the math, plan ahead, look at the surrounding boxes,
and figure out where the words are within the puzzle. Use these
tips in order to continue finding the rest of the words within the
puzzle.

Additional Tips

- Try to solve the math within the box to
  within the puzzle
- Try and look for letters that are not in oth
- In puzzles that have similar letters within w
  and find the letters that are the same (It some
  to look for a word backwards, starting with the
  letter in the word)
- Remember, you can only use a box once; so try an
  plan ahead

EASY

13+12	15+6	7+8	11+2	10+12	6+3	9+8
12+12	5+3	1+0	1+4	6+5	14+8	8+7
10+9	1+0	14+4	1+0	14+3	12+1	3+2
10+2	3+0	3+4	3+3	4+2	15+3	7+3
7+4	8+4	6+2	3+3	12+11	10+9	5+6
11+4	16+7	8+9	10+2	11+4	2+1	2+0
1+0	4+5	6+6	12+6	4+1	12+2	17+8

WORDS

1. ben AFFLECK
2. pooch HALL
3. allen IVERSON
4. chris MARCH

EASY

15+6	6+4	7+2	1+4	15+3	11+8	10+4
14+3	1+0	13+6	6+6	1+0	6+4	8+7
10+3	19+3	2+1	12+11	3+2	15+10	8+6
21+3	11+6	9+2	13+12	3+1	13+2	8+4
5+4	14+5	4+3	2+2	4+1	11+11	12+4
11+4	16+7	18+4	1+0	25+1	15+3	22+3
21+4	7+7	5+3	17+5	15+10	3+4	4+4

WORDS

1. deitrick HADDON
2. randy JACKSON
3. diane SAWYER
4. ron ISLEY

EASY

12+4	5+4	18+1	11+12	14+5	8+6	9+0
8+8	1+0	12+4	5+3	16+3	8+7	3+1
2+2	7+3	12+3	17+5	8+3	18+3	11+3
19+3	14+4	1+0	2+1	4+5	14+4	4+6
6+5	5+3	12+4	5+2	11+7	10+3	4+1
11+11	3+0	1+0	3+2	4+1	1+1	10+1
12+4	15+6	12+4	7+6	9+3	4+4	12+10

WORDS

1. jermaine JACKSON
2. nicholas CAGE
3. miranda KERR
4. marvin SAPP

EASY

6+5	12+7	18+3	3+1	15+3	4+4	12+3
1+3	4+5	1+0	7+6	12+10	1+0	11+11
14+5	10+8	15+8	15+5	12+8	16+1	5+3
17+2	1+0	4+1	10+5	3+3	7+5	4+3
17+8	12+10	2+1	6+1	3+2	11+12	1+0
21+3	24+0	15+4	4+3	1+0	6+4	1+1
13+3	5+5	17+5	7+4	5+7	10+10	12+4

WORDS

1. jill SCOTT
2. mick JAGGER
3. penny HARDAWAY
4. christian BALE

EASY

12+2	4+4	7+4	2+1	10+10	7+3	11+12
1+4	12+7	5+6	7+3	1+0	16+3	10+4
12+5	13+2	4+4	3+1	3+2	10+4	9+6
9+5	1+1	1+0	12+4	1+4	7+5	5+6
6+4	14+5	20+3	10+3	2+0	21+2	20+0
11+4	15+3	12+6	17+5	1+0	11+5	10+6
16+7	11+2	1+0	23+1	16+3	3+3	6+6

WORDS

1. dwayne WADE
2. petey PABLO
3. bruno MARS
4. janet JACKSON

EASY

15+5	7+6	10+11	9+2	4+1	11+3	17+3
12+4	1+1	1+0	10+4	16+1	12+6	1+1
21+3	2+3	4+5	7+7	6+2	10+6	2+6
7+6	8+7	18+3	12+4	10+11	14+1	9+1
11+12	3+2	8+6	12+2	14+5	1+5	7+4
16+7	5+4	10+6	9+7	1+0	18+3	19+1
5+2	12+2	12+12	3+3	4+1	4+2	6+5

WORDS

1. olivia n. JOHN
2. mike EPPS
3. tonya BAKER
4. dakota FANNING

EASY

14+4	5+6	7+1	12+12	15+4	11+4	16+4
21+0	4+1	12+2	7+2	13+5	16+9	4+3
2+2	2+1	12+5	2+1	6+5	10+10	3+2
12+4	1+6	5+4	7+5	7+8	9+2	10+1
12+11	3+4	11+11	24+1	1+1	4+6	7+1
12+5	5+6	7+5	7+6	8+8	13+3	10+9
10+3	11+4	16+3	14+7	1+0	18+3	12+12

WORDS

1. michael VICK
2. chris PAUL
3. alicia KEYS
4. robert DENIRO

EASY

10+10	1+4	8+2	5+3	12+4	10+10	3+1
9+3	5+2	1+0	4+4	1+0	11+9	3+3
12+12	2+1	4+1	16+4	13+4	16+3	15+6
7+4	11+3	15+3	3+2	17+3	7+6	18+3
11+8	10+3	12+3	17+3	7+7	10+3	19+2
13+2	11+9	11+4	21+0	13+5	4+1	22+2
2+2	10+4	1+1	8+7	12+5	5+6	7+5

WORDS

1. channing TATUM
2. julianne MOORE
3. richard GERE
4. phil JACKSON

14

EASY

15+6	7+6	10+3	19+2	5+3	8+1	2+2
14+2	4+5	4+4	12+12	17+2	1+1	1+0
3+4	7+2	7+5	1+0	17+3	6+3	13+1
18+2	10+10	16+4	2+2	16+2	11+3	12+4
16+3	11+9	11+7	3+3	3+1	18+3	19+3
3+2	1+0	12+12	5+6	7+2	1+0	6+4
6+6	7+4	4+1	6+6	1+1	10+10	19+2

WORDS

1. sue BIRD
2. brad PITT
3. idris ELBA
4. rob KARDASHIAN

EASY

6+6	7+1	12+10	3+4	2+1	4+4	17+8
6+3	4+3	2+0	1+0	5+5	12+12	12+3
16+3	1+0	17+2	8+5	19+3	7+7	17+4
21+0	11+1	10+6	22+2	7+2	12+2	5+3
3+3	1+1	3+1	10+13	13+5	6+1	12+7
5+5	3+2	10+4	15+6	7+3	1+0	19+4
10+2	8+4	16+9	23+1	12+4	3+1	14+3

WORDS

1. stacy DASH
2. alec BALDWIN
3. naomi CAMPBELL
4. vince YOUNG

EASY

12+10	4+3	5+5	18+3	19+3	12+12	1+0
14+5	17+3	3+2	11+4	13+1	12+5	16+2
6+5	6+6	10+10	6+1	10+3	11+3	4+1
15+4	16+4	5+3	1+0	7+3	15+3	7+7
13+3	1+0	8+8	9+3	2+1	10+5	17+2
19+4	12+4	6+4	7+3	10+12	6+3	2+2
15+5	14+5	2+2	1+0	4+2	4+1	11+3

WORDS

1. byron CAGE
2. viola DAVIS
3. paula PATTON
4. roger FEDORER

EASY

7+7	10+3	12+12	6+1	1+0	18+4	21+2
20+0	3+4	13+1	9+5	5+6	12+4	3+2
11+4	7+4	7+2	11+8	13+2	10+9	12+1
16+5	17+8	3+4	5+5	4+3	12+4	10+10
15+0	14+3	2+1	10+1	5+2	1+1	11+3
2+1	1+0	6+4	7+2	17+2	13+2	4+4
9+1	3+3	13+3	1+1	10+10	3+4	5+1

WORDS

1. jason BIGGS
2. gale KING
3. samuel l. JACKSON
4. chris EVANS

EASY

12+5	5+6	7+2	4+2	12+12	10+4	19+2
2+2	4+4	6+3	12+4	9+6	13+13	4+6
7+0	6+4	18+7	12+12	17+2	5+6	4+1
12+12	1+1	7+5	16+8	12+6	2+0	2+2
17+3	10+2	18+3	19+0	1+1	4+3	12+2
11+11	1+0	12+13	14+6	12+3	6+5	4+1
16+3	7+5	8+8	5+3	9+3	7+6	12+0

WORDS

1. john SALLY
2. darwin HOBBS
3. eva MENDEZ
4. jamie FOXX

EASY

12+10	3+2	5+5	11+1	16+7	7+8	10+10
7+4	11+4	16+5	15+3	3+2	16+4	3+3
5+5	3+2	12+4	11+12	9+5	11+11	15+3
4+0	7+7	14+0	14+1	12+5	1+0	18+3
12+4	21+3	7+7	14+7	22+3	5+4	6+2
12+10	3+4	6+5	4+1	2+2	7+6	10+11
1+1	5+2	8+1	6+6	8+4	20+5	1+0

WORDS

1. jay LENO
2. jamie KENNEDY
3. johnny GILL
4. kevin HART

EASY

3+4	5+1	13+2	12+12	1+0	5+5	7+6
10+10	12+3	4+3	10+8	5+5	5+4	10+11
11+12	1+1	1+0	15+4	3+1	9+2	18+3
19+3	11+5	16+6	17+2	11+8	1+0	4+1
1+1	1+0	6+2	14+5	4+3	10+4	4+4
11+3	5+6	13+2	14+1	6+6	17+2	18+2
4+3	15+4	18+1	5+5	12+2	6+6	18+4

WORDS

1. lance BASS
2. clay AIKEN
3. scarlett JOHANSSON
4. harrison FORD

EASY

5+5	6+1	15+3	12+1	16+2	1+1	4+1
3+3	5+6	3+3	3+2	7+6	14+4	11+1
10+10	11+5	17+1	11+12	13+4	7+5	5+3
5+5	1+1	5+4	3+1	3+2	10+10	19+2
2+2	10+13	3+2	2+1	1+0	20+2	7+2
15+1	7+2	4+1	23+1	7+7	12+7	16+3
1+1	12+8	15+4	9+8	10+11	10+13	5+4

WORDS

1. clive DAVIS
2. will FERRELL
3. kanye WEST
4. kelly PRICE

EASY

4+4	15+3	7+6	17+3	5+4	12+1	14+5
15+8	15+6	19+2	15+4	1+0	5+5	7+6
8+5	14+1	7+6	17+3	6+1	11+11	23+2
10+10	1+1	1+0	5+4	5+3	1+0	5+6
16+7	14+5	4+1	10+11	11+1	5+2	12+2
12+4	17+3	15+5	6+6	8+8	8+7	1+0
13+13	18+5	7+2	15+4	9+1	17+2	4+4

WORDS

1. lady GAGA
2. tim TEBOW
3. nick JONAS
4. pharell WILLIAMS

EASY

11+3	4+3	6+6	3+0	4+1	5+5	10+2
18+3	3+2	19+3	1+1	1+0	7+2	16+4
15+3	22+0	4+4	8+7	11+3	8+8	9+2
9+3	12+8	6+6	8+6	9+4	15+4	11+8
20+3	24+1	1+1	9+6	11+3	10+6	4+3
5+5	15+6	13+5	1+0	13+1	12+12	11+8
13+11	12+5	7+6	1+1	7+7	12+3	3+3

WORDS

1. nick CANNON
2. tina THOMPSON
3. keith URBAN
4. stacy KIEBLER

EASY

4+4	6+5	12+12	10+3	1+0	9+4	4+4
6+5	7+8	11+4	11+2	15+3	19+3	16+7
22+2	11+1	5+4	12+2	17+5	14+4	15+4
1+1	12+0	15+6	3+2	6+3	5+0	4+5
5+5	3+1	1+0	4+1	17+3	2+1	13+4
5+4	17+2	14+4	6+3	2+2	1+0	1+1
5+3	13+4	6+4	1+0	14+2	7+6	12+10

WORDS

1. keanu REEVES
2. al PACINO
3. damon DASH
4. adriana LIMA

EASY

14+3	1+1	13+3	12+5	7+6	8+8	2+2
1+0	1+3	1+0	4+5	6+4	1+0	12+12
7+4	13+10	10+8	11+8	6+2	5+2	11+10
4+1	15+3	11+3	12+6	16+4	7+2	4+1
17+2	6+5	4+1	4+4	12+2	3+3	5+4
16+7	8+4	12+4	8+6	8+4	5+2	3+1
1+1	5+2	16+4	8+8	11+4	12+8	14+2

WORDS

1. kerry WASHINGTON
2. steve KERR
3. ellen PAGE
4. spencer BAKER

EASY

1+1	13+4	4+3	17+4	8+8	2+1	10+10
15+3	11+12	8+3	14+7	11+10	4+4	4+3
1+1	4+1	10+2	10+4	1+0	17+2	16+0
15+4	7+8	6+3	3+1	12+2	3+2	17+8
4+5	7+3	12+7	8+5	8+6	9+5	10+3
12+9	1+1	3+2	6+6	14+1	1+0	21+2
20+2	22+1	12+12	6+4	9+3	5+3	2+2

WORDS

1. jim JONES
2. mila KUNIS
3. bill BELLAMY
4. tyson CHANDLER

EASY

4+4	15+3	11+12	9+7	15+6	12+10	10+10
4+3	1+0	5+6	3+2	7+3	1+0	4+4
12+12	21+4	12+6	7+7	4+1	13+3	7+5
16+3	1+0	16+2	3+2	9+6	11+2	17+2
7+7	4+2	19+2	2+2	15+3	1+0	20+4
10+9	16+4	10+12	4+4	11+11	4+1	11+3
4+3	15+6	10+9	12+1	15+5	5+3	1+1

WORDS

1. morgan FREEMAN
2. marlon WAYANS
3. cyndi LAUPER
4. charlize THERON

EASY

8+8	16+2	10+11	11+12	1+1	11+8	4+3
6+6	5+3	3+2	7+4	10+3	17+3	4+1
14+3	22+3	17+3	17+3	19+2	20+2	8+6
21+3	12+2	3+2	6+6	13+13	8+7	12+13
10+5	1+1	5+2	15+3	17+4	6+4	17+3
7+5	11+4	15+4	1+0	3+1	6+4	7+4
1+0	3+1	12+0	10+9	3+3	1+1	1+0

WORDS

1. bob SAGET
2. james JONES
3. paula ABDUL
4. ryan REYNOLDS

EASY

15-10	24-5	17-6	18-7	12-10	36-32	10-2
15-6	7-6	5-3	17-12	12-4	50-25	7-1
22-5	36-12	15-5	16-8	55-34	17-2	17-12
15-6	20-5	37-33	25-24	10-7	30-14	45-34
11-4	17-8	28-14	30-12	6-3	10-2	12-6
11-5	30-7	7-2	26-13	17-4	12-7	12-8
18-9	25-6	12-11	25-7	14-7	10-3	16-3

WORDS

1. colt MCCOY
2. bobby JONES
3. joy BEHAR
4. gavin DEGRAW

EASY

24-12	16-14	10-5	26-21	47-22	45-34	18-9
10-2	13-12	24-2	18-13	17-4	18-9	18-12
12-4	16-7	20-0	25-16	13-10	22-3	25-10
10-7	20-7	38-29	15-10	25-6	19-1	30-12
12-4	25-22	17-14	67-45	17-3	15-10	10-5
17-4	14-8	16-13	27-18	20-11	16-2	26-13
10-2	25-16	27-3	14-13	30-14	15-14	28-10

WORDS

1. paul PIERCE
2. john MCCAIN
3. kathy BATES
4. george FOREMAN

EASY

46-20	35-23	16-4	17-5	10-2	17-3	22-12
16-7	19-8	30-11	20-0	44-35	75-50	56-47
25-12	47-28	66-55	10-9	15-10	27-9	13-5
25-2	12-4	13-4	44-22	19-14	10-3	10-5
16-12	55-36	14-13	28-10	20-18	30-16	16-8
32-24	54-34	22-11	20-12	42-28	7-4	17-2
5-3	12-2	20-5	42-21	25-5	20-1	16-7

WORDS

1. swiss BEATS
2. ashton KUTCHER
3. steve HARVEY
4. michael JOHNSON

EASY

45-30	38-19	14-9	44-22	17-7	14-6	64-45
56-47	25-14	43-33	16-2	23-8	20-13	20-17
15-3	24-12	20-14	44-33	29-10	11-10	6-3
12-4	10-9	24-10	20-8	25-6	26-13	7-4
17-5	18-5	25-16	17-16	36-23	18-13	47-38
21-15	25-10	56-47	12-9	42-28	66-57	36-18
34-12	26-22	13-10	17-8	19-10	45-30	4-1

WORDS

1. joe FLACCO
2. candace CAMERON
3. star JONES
4. tom HANKS

EASY

44-20	16-7	27-12	15-5	26-17	24-12	18-6
10-2	42-28	18-7	45-36	20-7	25-10	44-33
16-7	25-24	17-15	12-7	18-5	23-4	25-5
29-7	24-12	27-8	18-9	48-32	29-4	16-3
17-8	22-16	34-25	37-26	30-14	20-19	17-6
40-24	45-24	16-5	20-11	24-4	10-5	33-22
5-4	46-23	16-8	8-2	7-2	16-12	9-3

WORDS

1. johnny DEPP
2. kevin JONAS
3. marisa TOMEI
4. barry WHITE

EASY

7-3	12-5	10-6	12-7	44-35	50-25	36-22
14-2	17-6	30-12	22-12	12-6	36-18	34-10
35-23	18-9	12-7	12-1	15-14	35-30	18-7
25-6	27-7	22-12	21-14	30-9	24-6	44-33
50-25	56-46	66-47	15-10	26-17	13-10	11-10
11-4	24-10	29-10	5-4	19-14	12-10	8-1
12-9	7-3	30-7	14-13	17-9	27-7	29-4

WORDS

1. bob SEGER
2. anita BAKER
3. goldie HAWN
4. farrah FAUCET

35

EASY

35-10	30-16	44-35	30-18	16-7	54-36	24-12
15-10	35-33	10-9	56-47	17-12	55-33	15-4
17-5	10-3	18-10	7-3	26-13	16-4	12-7
11-4	23-22	25-16	28-4	10-6	24-12	19-4
17-12	15-2	18-12	24-10	16-5	16-15	25-20
3-1	16-7	30-17	26-7	30-14	28-9	18-9
12-4	54-36	67-46	17-7	45-30	36-24	25-15

WORDS

1. keke PALMER
2. mia HAMM
3. angelina JOLIE
4. diane LANE

EASY

35-20	20-18	35-30	16-7	18-9	33-20	16-15
25-12	55-44	30-21	18-9	24-12	25-21	16-8
14-5	17-8	14-10	12-10	18-13	30-11	5-2
8-3	15-10	9-3	18-14	10-2	14-13	11-6
17-8	30-16	12-8	24-10	25-11	27-2	28-19
14-10	16-5	14-13	20-11	11-3	26-8	18-9
26-7	29-23	26-13	30-22	15-10	45-27	44-20

WORDS

1. niecey NASH
2. tara REID
3. joe BIDEN
4. howie MANDEL

EASY

45-36	77-66	18-12	48-36	15-14	30-8	15-6
26-8	29-10	45-36	17-3	45-30	5-1	18-7
19-2	18-14	17-10	56-37	44-33	38-19	33-20
15-7	5-1	17-12	8-1	9-5	30-10	45-36
55-40	16-3	11-10	8-2	10-9	19-12	75-50
13-5	30-17	17-8	20-6	46-23	17-12	17-10
3-1	15-7	14-13	25-7	36-24	20-4	27-18

WORDS

1. emma WATSON
2. bob MARLEY
3. ester DEAN
4. flavor FLAV

EASY

17-7	25-10	19-12	66-55	21-16	27-18	20-3
60-45	18-9	27-12	45-30	20-19	26-7	44-24
24-16	14-11	50-25	17-13	55-35	44-33	37-26
20-6	20-16	11-10	45-26	20-10	33-23	28-14
23-10	25-6	30-12	6-1	30-15	17-16	10-7
19-11	16-1	29-12	40-20	15-10	12-10	13-5
6-1	14-0	7-4	15-10	28-10	21-15	27-16

WORDS

1. tyra BANKS
2. aaron CARTER
3. boris KODJOE
4. dewayne JOHNSON

EASY

26-16	33-20	16-7	18-8	36-18	22-15	10-5
19-12	38-19	12-6	11-10	20-16	28-10	24-12
25-16	45-37	17-12	30-18	55-44	30-12	20-8
36-27	45-33	16-5	42-35	33-10	20-5	10-2
18-10	33-22	24-10	45-30	30-16	7-2	15-9
17-8	15-10	22-11	27-18	21-14	17-2	13-2
15-12	11-5	17-3	25-10	22-10	29-25	26-25

WORDS

1. melyssa FORD
2. coretta s. KING
3. colin FARRELL
4. beyonce KNOWLES

EASY

16-12	33-12	20-16	16-4	30-17	28-19	24-16
33-22	14-13	30-12	17-12	27-21	39-26	16-15
28-19	44-22	10-5	45-36	55-33	16-3	18-7
10-2	17-8	20-15	18-9	25-11	22-19	26-13
29-24	12-8	36-24	25-10	14-11	56-47	30-15
33-14	25-6	18-17	17-3	21-15	22-18	22-16
20-14	32-16	17-2	15-3	45-30	6-4	16-2

WORDS

1. sarah PALIN
2. lamar ODOM
3. mc HAMMER
4. tommy DAVISON

EASY

15-7	10-3	27-15	45-25	66-55	26-21	12-10
17-8	19-12	13-10	15-10	13-5	18-7	42-35
26-21	27-22	36-18	28-14	4-3	26-12	25-11
18-6	10-5	14-13	11-6	48-32	17-2	27-18
25-17	18-6	44-24	25-7	24-21	30-11	30-16
35-22	12-4	17-16	47-27	75-50	42-28	45-34
16-7	11-3	7-3	25-5	15-14	20-7	4-1

WORDS

1. mike TYSON
2. john CENA
3. hill HARPER
4. eli MANNING

42

EASY

16-7	27-10	25-16	67-57	25-14	43-24	15-5
17-4	11-8	23-10	30-11	11-2	18-9	45-30
25-14	25-6	45-36	18-9	55-44	32-24	50-25
65-46	24-14	11-2	25-15	36-18	10-2	30-16
16-8	39-29	46-23	33-20	28-10	21-14	38-19
3-1	18-13	15-3	27-18	16-2	45-30	30-15
12-7	30-18	27-18	33-22	18-9	24-10	25-11

WORDS

1. chuck NORRIS
2. leona LEWIS
3. larry KING
4. michael JOHNSON

EASY

44-35	26-17	20-12	30-15	30-25	50-25	25-12
11-5	6-3	30-14	15-1	16-4	66-55	18-9
12-3	55-46	60-45	11-10	30-12	46-27	28-14
25-16	17-9	26-6	29-10	10-2	19-4	45-30
11-6	17-8	24-5	25-23	18-14	23-10	19-17
45-35	14-13	22-13	14-10	18-17	55-33	13-12
17-8	14-11	16-4	28-21	20-4	26-4	28-7

WORDS

1. rosa PARK
2. matt DAMON
3. johnny CASH
4. mel GIBSON

EASY

45-30	55-46	30-5	13-5	17-8	18-13	34-20
16-7	20-5	25-7	16-3	23-9	12-4	30-18
17-8	19-12	20-14	30-12	20-11	36-24	25-17
45-36	33-22	15-10	5-1	26-21	22-21	14-8
18-6	30-14	24-11	25-23	46-34	23-0	50-25
46-34	24-12	12-11	34-12	27-7	36-18	11-10
13-6	16-8	17-11	30-15	22-8	15-11	11-1

WORDS

1. mark TWAIN
2. katy PERRY
3. jane FONDA
4. patti LABELLE

45

EASY

25-16	22-16	14-11	24-10	14-2	32-24	17-8
34-25	55-46	27-26	65-46	25-24	17-8	32-16
10-2	30-12	24-11	26-7	26-13	34-19	25-10
22-16	36-18	45-35	44-33	39-26	23-11	7-4
13-8	17-4	10-1	45-30	26-25	48-36	45-35
27-23	14-12	24-12	10-4	42-28	19-15	27-8
29-10	28-11	26-4	18-9	28-21	15-10	33-12

WORDS

1. kevin POLLAK
2. kurt CARR
3. mary j. BLIGE
4. fred HAMMOND

EASY

15-7	10-2	18-9	22-6	28-17	29-21	19-14
18-15	20-2	26-10	29-10	22-17	25-7	17-3
12-6	15-10	26-12	32-24	21-4	60-45	11-3
40-20	60-45	34-23	20-15	28-23	54-45	30-17
24-10	30-7	11-10	24-12	29-24	20-16	100-75
17-10	27-18	34-24	42-28	44-33	36-18	16-4
48-32	20-16	18-16	10-9	30-12	17-9	10-7

WORDS

1. charlie SHEEN
2. paul WALKER
3. drew BARRYMORE
4. freida PINTO

EASY

16-7	12-5	25-6	30-18	10-6	16-7	26-3
28-19	22-17	45-35	30-12	17-12	10-3	18-9
25-10	24-10	16-11	26-10	46-23	24-22	30-16
21-13	13-11	17-13	16-11	16-7	26-17	24-23
17-12	16-15	14-6	42-28	26-4	38-19	32-24
20-13	28-5	20-7	12-11	11-2	25-14	16-8
10-6	12-11	46-25	55-44	30-11	24-20	45-34

WORDS

1. barack OBAMA
2. blake LEWIS
3. chaka KHAN
4. deion SANDERS

EASY

25-10	46-36	42-21	55-47	24-10	30-10	18-9
22-12	16-2	28-7	29-10	20-19	26-17	14-9
21-17	17-13	28-17	30-14	14-10	36-24	6-2
22-18	4-1	15-10	22-10	7-3	24-10	26-25
33-20	14-7	20-2	45-36	13-2	15-4	24-16
16-7	33-10	28-14	15-6	10-3	13-10	25-11
10-4	45-30	75-60	4-0	44-33	56-46	17-14

WORDS

1. dev PATEL
2. martin l. KING
3. jackie CHAN
4. carrie UNDERWOOD

EASY

22-17	16-14	17-7	10-6	42-28	24-14	38-19
46-37	14-13	44-33	45-30	26-8	17-16	30-15
40-35	14-11	30-12	16-2	30-15	17-8	29-14
27-23	26-15	32-24	55-44	10-3	24-12	3-1
12-6	18-3	10-5	10-5	36-24	75-50	55-45
50-25	19-0	27-3	25-20	16-15	56-51	14-5
26-13	27-10	16-2	25-5	26-1	28-14	30-5

WORDS

1. elizabeth TAYLOR
2. kenny CHESNEY
3. joe JONAS
4. charles BARKLEY

EASY

45-30	55-35	14-5	26-17	45-30	30-18	34-29
10-3	19-7	15-7	40-20	22-16	30-16	30-11
27-18	19-8	34-20	10-9	11-6	25-5	24-10
33-13	23-10	11-6	47-28	45-34	15-10	45-25
11-4	34-23	6-3	8-2	16-10	30-8	60-45
11-6	45-35	67-47	21-14	20-11	66-44	13-10
25-6	44-33	23-9	14-13	13-11	21-14	29-10

WORDS

1. diane KEATON
2. robin GIVENS
3. lloyd BANKS
4. seann w. SCOTT

EASY

23-0	15-0	16-0	18-0	22-0	25-0	16-0
3-0	13-0	5-0	11-0	18-0	14-0	2-0
17-0	16-0	18-0	12-0	25-0	4-0	15-0
22-0	19-0	26-0	17-0	9-0	21-0	19-0
11-0	6-0	5-0	4-0	5-0	14-0	3-0
2-0	12-0	11-0	18-0	22-0	21-0	1-0
20-0	23-0	5-0	1-0	24-0	15-0	13-0

WORDS

1. la REID
2. tyler PERRY
3. nene LEAKES
4. marilyn MANSON

EASY

2X1	3X6	2X10	2X7	3X1	4X5	12X2
3X6	3X5	1X1	3X5	2X2	3X7	8X3
23X1	3X4	5X5	19X1	2X3	4X2	12X2
10X2	11X2	4X6	1X1	2X1	1X1	2X7
12X1	2X6	17X1	5X5	2X9	3X5	2X10
3X6	1X1	3X5	1X1	2X2	4X4	3X4
2X8	4X5	2X9	2X7	2X11	3X5	9X2

WORDS

1. bill COSBY
2. lauren LONDON
3. kelly ROWLAND
4. john TRAVOLTA

EASY

2X1	3X3	2X10	5X1	2X7	3X5	6X2
6X3	12X2	4X2	2X6	11X1	2X9	2X2
5X2	1X1	5X3	19X1	5X1	3X3	5X1
3X6	4X5	17X1	3X5	3X4	2X5	4X5
4X2	11X1	23X1	3X5	2X7	2X9	3X8
4X6	1X1	3X1	5X5	8X3	3X5	3X7
3X3	23X1	1X1	6X3	2X8	6X4	5X2

WORDS

1. natalie COLE
2. kim PORTER
3. lalah HATHAWAY
4. wille NELSON

EASY

2X7	3X3	12X2	19X1	4X5	2X7	5X5
3X6	10X2	21X1	23X1	3X5	2X11	2X4
3X3	3X5	3X1	17X1	4X5	2X9	3X3
3X6	17X1	19X1	23X1	2X10	3X3	3X5
3X8	3X2	19X1	1X1	5X1	12X2	3X2
13X2	2X2	1X1	4X3	2X7	3X3	1X1
19X1	2X10	3X7	4X4	3X6	2X4	2X11

WORDS

1. wayne NEWTON
2. diana ROSS
3. jermaine DUPRI
4. queen LATIFAH

EASY

3X3	2X7	5X1	2X7	3X4	5X3	5X4
5X5	2X4	1X1	6X3	19X1	17X1	2X2
3X1	13X2	13X1	3X5	19X1	2X2	12X2
2X11	2X2	13X1	2X2	2X9	5X1	19X1
3X8	2X7	17X1	1X1	3X5	5X1	2X2
3X2	3X5	3X7	23X1	3X5	13X2	2X7
13X1	2X4	3X5	2X1	7X1	2X2	3X5

WORDS

1. liam NEESOM
2. dwight HOWARD
3. john GOODMAN
4. gisele BUNDCHEN

EASY

2X11	2X10	4X4	3X3	2X10	3X5	2X7
3X6	4X4	1X1	3X5	2X6	4X3	12X2
4X2	2X1	3X7	5X1	5X5	3X3	13X2
17X1	2X9	5X5	2X4	5X1	2X4	2X8
8X3	1X1	2X7	3X4	4X4	3X6	5X5
19X1	6X3	6X4	5X1	12X2	13X1	19X1
17X1	3X3	19X1	19X1	1X1	2X10	14X1

WORDS

1. paris HILTON
2. amanda BYNES
3. amy POEHLER
4. diana TAURASI

EASY

3X4	5X4	12X1	19X1	17X1	2X2	3X2
3X3	4X4	3X6	10X2	2X11	5X5	2X9
5X4	1X1	19X1	5X5	5X3	5X1	11X2
3X4	3X6	3X5	13X2	4X5	4X6	17X1
3X7	7X1	2X3	3X4	2X1	1X1	4X4
3X5	2X2	5X5	3X5	1X1	3X5	10X2
3X4	5X1	3X4	17X1	23X1	19X1	23X1

WORDS

1. barbara WALTER
2. richard PRYOR
3. rebecca LOBO
4. michael DOUGLAS

EASY

3X7	7X2	12X2	2X9	1X1	19X1	2X1
11X2	10X2	7X1	5X5	2X7	5X3	4X4
2X2	2X10	19X1	4X5	3X3	19X1	4X5
3X2	5X1	2X4	2X2	13X1	2X7	2X9
5X5	2X2	3X7	3X6	5X3	1X1	5X2
2X7	2X9	23X1	1X1	11X1	2X2	19X1
2X1	1X1	13X1	3X3	3X2	10X2	1X1

WORDS

1. yolanda ADAMS
2. hugh GRANT
3. john EDWARDS
4. uma THURMAN

EASY

17X1	3X1	3X5	3X5	3X6	2X4	5X5
5X2	11X1	3X6	4X4	5X1	3X3	2X11
2X2	3X2	3X5	3X3	3X4	2X9	15X1
3X6	3X5	3X6	2X1	5X1	19X1	17X1
23X1	3X2	4X6	5X1	3X8	2X9	3X5
2X7	1X1	5X5	2X2	3X5	4X5	2X7
4X4	3X3	23X1	4X3	19X1	3X4	10X2

WORDS

1. julia ROBERTS
2. keri HILSON
3. cynthia COOPER
4. oprah WINFREY

EASY

3X2	12X2	2X7	1X1	10X2	2X7	11X2
23X1	19X1	4X6	5X5	5X3	2X2	3X3
1X1	3X5	23X1	5X5	3X3	3X2	4X4
3X5	3X7	6X4	2X4	3X4	2X2	3X2
12X2	2X8	10X2	2X6	4X4	3X6	3X3
2X2	19X1	3X7	3X6	1X1	19X1	2X9
24X1	23X1	3X3	13X1	5X5	5X3	7X1

WORDS

1. ricky DILLARD
2. sheryl SWOOPS
3. brittany MURPHY
4. blake GRIFFIN

61

EASY

19X1	2X11	3X3	4X5	3X4	12X2	3X7
17X1	4X5	2X10	3X3	7X2	3X5	7X1
11X1	3X7	5X1	2X2	1X1	4X4	5X5
5X3	19X1	2X2	5X1	19X1	3X6	5X1
2X10	19X1	3X4	2X6	23X1	2X2	13X2
4X3	4X4	1X1	17X1	3X5	21X1	23X1
4X6	3X3	8X3	2X1	19X1	3X1	20X1

WORDS

1. ruben STUDDARD
2. jennifer LOPEZ
3. angela BASSETT
4. simon COWELL

EASY

19X1	2X10	3X5	2X2	2X5	12X2	3X3
4X3	7X1	5X5	2X9	11X1	13X1	17X1
4X4	7X1	5X2	1X1	2X8	2X2	3X3
3X4	19X1	3X3	17X1	2X4	8X3	3X1
13X2	2X9	2X7	5X5	5X3	2X4	9X2
9X1	3X5	5X1	4X5	3X3	5X1	5X1
2X7	13X1	19X1	3X4	23X1	4X4	12X1

WORDS

1. curtis PAINTER
2. lea MICHELE
3. snoop DOGG
4. gretchen WILSON

EASY

2X11	19X1	3X3	2X2	3X6	3X3	10X2
19X1	17X1	2X8	5X1	4X4	5X5	22X1
5X2	2X1	3X6	1X1	2X9	17X1	5X1
3X1	19X1	5X1	4X3	23X1	2X9	4X2
12X2	13X2	2X7	19X1	2X1	3X5	3X1
3X3	2X7	4X4	5X1	12X2	13X1	10X2
4X5	2X10	5X1	2X11	23X1	3X8	3X3

WORDS

1. tia MOWRY
2. tony BENNETT
3. minnie DRIVER
4. britney SPEARS

EASY

12X2	2X2	3X3	4X5	10X2	1X1	11X2
2X7	23X1	19X1	17X1	3X4	2X7	2X8
3X3	1X1	10X2	3X7	5X5	2X1	3X6
5X3	2X6	5X4	13X1	1X1	5X1	19X1
4X2	2X9	5X1	4X3	13X1	3X3	13X1
17X1	19X1	3X5	4X4	3X5	2X7	3X8
4X6	6X3	5X1	19X1	2X1	3X1	2X2

WORDS

1. donna SUMMERS
2. amber ROSE
3. jessica ALBA
4. kenneth COPELAND

65

EASY

2X2	13X2	5X1	2X7	2X2	4X5	3X8
19X1	3X1	2X11	2X6	3X4	2X10	1X1
3X3	3X5	5X1	2X2	3X1	1X1	23X1
15X1	19X1	3X4	2X1	3X4	2X4	1X1
5X5	11X1	2X11	5X1	19X1	9X2	2X10
2X8	14X1	2X10	1X1	2X9	5X5	2X7
13X2	17X1	19X1	7X1	11X1	19X1	3X5

WORDS

1. david COOK
2. tim ALLEN
3. cicely TYSON
4. mark WAHLBERG

EASY

12X2	13X2	19X1	1X1	17X1	13X1	4X4
6X3	5X5	3X6	3X2	2X6	3X7	2X2
3X4	2X4	13X1	5X1	2X9	3X4	7X1
13X1	3X7	3X6	19X1	4X4	2X7	5X5
12X2	2X9	2X2	2X10	3X5	2X4	4X3
3X7	3X8	19X1	2X9	3X3	2X8	2X9
2X11	2X1	2X10	3X5	2X7	10X2	13X1

WORDS

1. charlie MURPHY
2. kate HUDSON
3. bj ARMSTRONG
4. kim BURRELL

EASY

2X1	19X1	2X11	3X1	23X1	2X10	3X3
4X4	2X8	5X4	3X5	5X5	23X1	2X2
2X1	3X3	12X2	13X2	3X5	1X1	13X1
5X1	17X1	2X4	5X1	4X4	3X4	19X1
2X6	2X3	2X9	19X1	10X2	4X4	2X6
5X5	2X1	5X1	3X7	5X3	4X3	5X1
13X1	17X1	2X1	3X6	7X1	2X7	19X1

WORDS

1. reggie BUSH
2. rance ALLEN
3. anderson COOPER
4. steven SPIELBERG

EASY

19X1	2X10	2X1	3X1	3X3	5X5	2X6
4X4	23X1	4X5	2X4	23X1	13X1	5X1
17X1	19X1	3X3	2X2	1X1	3X5	4X5
1X1	12X2	3X2	13X2	4X4	2X10	3X5
3X3	4X3	5X5	4X5	3X4	5X1	2X9
3X7	19X1	2X7	3X3	3X6	5X1	17X1
2X11	17X1	2X7	1X1	13X1	2X10	3X1

WORDS

1. taylor SWIFT
2. demi MOORE
3. charlie CHAPLIN
4. david LETTERMAN

69

EASY

12X2	13X1	8X2	17X1	5X1	19X1	23X1
19X1	2X10	3X5	2X11	1X1	2X6	3X1
3X3	1X1	2X2	3X6	2X2	3X2	3X4
5X5	5X3	2X7	2X10	1X1	4X4	3X3
4X6	3X7	2X2	2X11	13X1	3X5	12X2
11X2	3X4	11X1	1X1	3X3	2X10	13X1
13X2	5X1	3X6	19X1	2X7	17X1	4X5

WORDS

1. miles DAVIS
2. adam SANDLER
3. missy ELLIOTT
4. natalie PORTMAN

70

EASY

4X4	2X4	3X4	5X1	5X5	17X1	19X1
23X1	2X8	3X3	2X6	7X1	1X1	2X2
4X4	4X2	17X1	5X5	4X5	3X5	4X5
13X1	1X1	5X3	5X1	13X2	2X7	5X1
9X2	3X7	12X2	3X3	19X1	1X1	4X4
2X2	2X1	9X1	23X1	3X5	5X1	23X1
17X1	19X1	3X7	2X1	2X6	3X6	23X1

WORDS

1. derrick ROSE
2. perez HILTON
3. michael BUBLE
4. christina APPLEGATE

EASY

2X10	2X11	3X3	2X7	4X4	5X3	5X5
2X7	17X1	19X1	2X2	3X5	3X6	12X2
11X2	2X6	1X1	2X7	19X1	5X1	1X1
13X1	19X1	3X5	3X3	4X5	2X7	11X1
3X1	13X2	3X1	3X6	1X1	3X7	2X9
5X4	5X5	3X2	2X7	2X9	3X5	1X1
10X2	19X1	2X6	3X3	17X1	4X4	13X1

WORDS

1. juelz SANTANA
2. abraham LINCOLN
3. candace PARKER
4. matthew MORRISON

EASY

3X3	4X4	12X2	13X1	1X1	17X1	19X1
23X1	13X1	3X7	13X2	3X2	2X2	5X5
5X3	3X2	2X2	2X9	3X2	5X1	9X1
13X1	23X1	3X6	4X4	3X4	2X10	23X1
12X2	11X2	2X4	5X1	3X3	5X1	12X2
3X8	4X4	5X5	2X8	2X4	3X1	5X3
3X1	3X5	3X5	23X1	13X2	17X1	11X1

WORDS

1. jessica WHITE
2. eddie MURPHY
3. casey AFFLECK
4. bradley COOPER

EASY

2X2	3X5	3X4	2X1	4X4	10X2	12X2
13X1	17X1	3X4	19X1	3X6	3X2	13X2
1X1	3X1	5X1	5X1	3X5	7X2	2X2
5X2	19X1	2X11	2X7	23X1	5X5	3X5
14X1	5X1	4X4	3X6	13X2	2X7	19X1
3X1	2X9	1X1	4X4	3X7	4X2	2X1
4X5	2X2	3X3	2X2	5X1	3X5	10X2

WORDS

1. chris BROWN
2. david SPADE
3. gerald LEVERT
4. sharon OSBOURNE

EASY

11X2	2X2	3X3	1X1	2X6	3X8	2X9
3X6	17X1	19X1	5X1	23X1	5X1	4X4
12X2	13X2	3X6	2X2	19X1	1X1	4X3
3X4	5X5	5X3	5X1	11X2	2X9	10X2
19X1	1X1	2X7	17X1	11X1	5X5	3X8
23X1	13X1	5X1	3X1	2X9	2X8	4X2
5X5	2X9	3X5	23X1	5X1	13X2	23X1

WORDS

1. sarah j. PARKER
2. tamara MOWRY
3. vin DIESEL
4. donald LAWRENCE

75

EASY

144/12	12/12	60/3	48/12	81/9	121/11	56/9
63/9	24/6	20/5	32/16	20/10	49/7	25/5
48/3	32/32	57/3	22/11	100/5	44/2	22/11
36/9	39/3	12/12	40/2	44/44	121/11	45/9
76/4	72/9	28/2	72/8	42/3	15/3	12/6
25/5	9/3	60/5	38/2	39/13	54/3	24/2
81/9	26/2	10/5	36/3	30/6	3/3	144/12

WORDS

1. ben STILLER
2. faith EVANS
3. amy ADAMS
4. donovan MCNABB

EASY

15/3	256/16	44/4	36/2	45/9	44/11	75/3
14/7	38/2	25/5	54/3	42/3	48/16	35/7
12/6	9/3	72/6	14/14	30/5	42/3	42/6
64/8	48/4	28/2	76/4	48/3	30/2	72/8
100/10	54/6	34/34	42/3	38/2	1/1	45/3
26/2	20/10	25/5	36/4	24/6	24/2	56/9
66/6	72/8	46/2	144/12	12/4	60/4	30/6

WORDS

1. jordin SPARKS
2. reggie MILLER
3. george CLOONEY
4. cece WINANS

EASY

46/2	49/7	46/2	14/2	28/7	25/5	225/15
144/12	28/2	72/8	45/3	45/5	54/3	57/3
100/10	55/11	81/9	45/9	64/8	54/3	39/3
100/4	32/4	42/3	36/12	44/4	11/11	42/2
9/3	12/3	16/4	75/5	63/7	16/4	49/7
81/9	121/11	45/5	60/3	60/5	32/8	25/5
30/5	46/2	19/1	84/7	16/4	49/7	169/13

WORDS

1. emma STONE
2. paul RUDD
3. robert DOWNEY
4. vanessa WILLIAMS

EASY

55/5	100/5	75/5	60/3	48/4	36/3	15/3
33/3	28/2	39/3	81/9	48/2	27/9	81/9
121/11	12/4	72/8	32/4	33/33	76/4	15/5
21/7	28/2	15/5	54/6	46/2	36/2	12/6
88/8	45/3	72/9	36/2	14/14	144/12	15/15
54/3	34/17	36/6	42/2	54/3	42/3	16/4
42/2	12/4	64/8	46/2	44/4	11/1	26/13

WORDS

1. hillary SWANK
2. rickey MINOR
3. toni BRAXTON
4. winston CHURCHILL

EASY

144/12	42/3	25/5	42/6	75/5	9/3	42/3
60/3	66/6	45/3	60/5	100/10	45/3	55/5
81/9	72/9	36/3	76/4	13/13	48/12	38/2
72/12	84/7	42/2	54/6	64/8	39/3	42/3
90/5	22/11	16/4	48/8	121/11	14/14	32/4
25/25	11/11	60/4	22/1	16/8	30/2	36/12
26/2	55/11	45/3	12/3	45/3	34/17	100/10

WORDS

1. michelle OBAMA
2. sandra BULLOCK
3. holly MADISON
4. levi JOHNSON

EASY

21/3	35/7	100/10	99/11	56/7	76/4	45/3
60/5	48/12	49/7	36/6	35/7	24/8	52/2
12/2	28/2	144/12	42/3	34/34	20/4	54/3
76/4	60/4	63/7	45/3	72/12	39/3	100/5
75/3	60/3	32/32	28/2	50/5	52/2	30/2
35/7	46/2	75/3	34/34	40/5	45/9	42/6
40/2	38/2	9/3	10/2	48/3	12/6	18/9

WORDS

1. catherine z. JONES
2. garry PAYTON
3. selena GOMEZ
4. shania TWAIN

EASY

22/11	30/6	39/13	28/2	30/2	72/8	42/2
75/5	12/12	81/9	20/5	24/3	80/4	42/3
26/2	72/8	24/2	121/11	54/3	42/3	144/12
25/5	57/3	54/3	48/4	26/2	8/8	32/32
24/2	45/5	400/20	54/6	25/5	12/2	75/3
9/3	27/9	46/2	21/3	32/4	54/3	49/7
30/5	63/7	64/8	38/2	90/18	14/7	11/11

WORDS

1. montel WILLIAMS
2. joy BRYANT
3. karen c. SHEARD
4. gabrielle UNION

EASY

35/7	45/3	60/5	12/2	66/6	64/8	90/5
42/3	39/3	24/12	50/10	13/13	54/6	46/2
35/7	169/13	81/9	196/14	36/2	54/3	81/9
14/7	46/2	24/6	20/1	45/3	54/6	72/6
27/9	60/3	80/4	21/7	39/3	48/4	27/27
60/12	72/6	60/4	25/5	84/7	30/2	26/2
25/5	24/3	42/3	22/11	144/12	15/3	57/3

WORDS

1. tony ROMO
2. cam NEWTON
3. carmen ELECTRA
4. wendy WILLIAMS

EASY

72/9	81/9	45/3	12/4	12/12	39/3	90/5
60/12	28/2	40/2	16/4	21/3	28/2	48/3
32/4	24/6	54/6	76/4	45/3	63/9	24/12
84/12	60/4	144/12	38/2	49/7	169/13	25/5
32/4	100/10	42/2	36/3	42/3	60/5	45/3
66/6	12/4	42/6	36/4	27/3	57/3	48/4
54/3	32/4	36/9	66/6	46/2	121/11	12/12

WORDS

1. charlie WILSON
2. julianne HOUGH
3. tisha CAMPBELL
4. sean KINGSTON

EASY

48/4	42/2	72/8	38/2	45/3	28/2	90/18
77/7	42/6	54/3	42/3	40/8	26/2	15/3
144/12	15/3	13/13	25/5	30/5	23/23	36/12
72/12	64/8	39/3	54/3	14/14	63/7	40/2
169/13	24/6	16/8	24/24	21/7	26/2	57/3
54/6	11/11	12/3	88/11	9/3	19/1	42/6
44/4	15/5	16/8	45/3	35/7	121/11	6/2

WORDS

1. nicole KIDMAN
2. john STAMOS
3. jj ABRAMS
4. tom GREENE

EASY

25/5	36/9	64/8	121/11	144/12	18/6	12/3
60/12	10/5	72/6	81/9	30/2	45/3	100/5
28/2	20/5	36/2	30/6	60/4	35/7	45/5
26/26	169/13	17/17	77/7	144/12	256/16	66/6
39/3	20/5	45/9	100/10	15/15	15/5	25/5
40/8	42/7	75/3	100/4	72/8	90/18	9/3
42/6	48/12	20/4	32/4	12/3	48/6	72/8

WORDS

1. andy DICK
2. tom BRADY
3. dane COOK
4. hugh HEFMAN

EASY

289/17	25/5	24/6	72/6	44/4	144/12	100/10
76/4	81/9	64/8	45/3	42/3	60/5	18/3
60/4	20/4	72/12	36/4	49/7	36/2	24/4
32/4	12/6	39/3	44/2	10/2	20/20	28/2
15/5	256/16	14/14	225/15	35/7	44/4	38/2
18/9	60/6	18/6	14/7	60/5	32/2	48/4
36/12	36/4	121/11	45/9	48/3	72/8	28/2

WORDS

1. harvey LEVIN
2. lebron JAMES
3. omar EPPS
4. aretha FRANKLIN

EASY

54/3	441/21	42/6	28/2	121/11	25/5	35/5
38/2	81/9	57/3	100/10	14/14	56/8	64/8
12/12	28/7	76/4	25/5	21/7	63/7	80/4
60/5	36/3	72/12	26/2	42/3	28/2	12/4
6/3	28/7	45/9	66/6	144/12	27/3	42/2
21/7	26/2	12/4	72/8	75/5	40/8	16/4
84/12	144/12	169/13	32/4	40/5	76/4	225/15

WORDS

1. katie HOLMES
2. brian MCKNIGHT
3. tim DUNCAN
4. brooke SHIELDS

EASY

144/12	38/2	39/3	15/3	32/8	100/10	121/11
169/13	42/6	60/12	2/2	38/2	60/4	100/5
400/20	34/34	15/3	18/2	44/4	60/3	38/2
27/9	36/2	24/2	42/3	30/2	75/5	21/7
24/8	44/2	25/5	60/5	81/9	64/8	60/4
256/16	54/6	27/3	32/2	48/8	35/5	36/2
54/3	46/2	39/3	44/4	48/2	100/10	12/6

WORDS

1. sharon STONE
2. naya RIVERA
3. garth BROOKS
4. serena WILLIAMS

EASY

48/6	25/5	48/12	441/21	45/9	54/3	46/2
529/23	30/2	46/2	76/4	10/5	45/5	18/6
12/4	144/12	54/9	169/13	60/3	48/4	22/22
100/10	81/9	57/3	48/8	24/2	64/8	20/4
72/12	12/3	84/7	81/9	26/2	12/12	38/2
15/15	225/15	27/3	56/8	3/3	256/16	18/9
121/11	45/3	60/5	42/3	63/9	38/2	88/8

WORDS

1. bruce WILLIS
2. philip HOFFMAN
3. taye DIGGS
4. ryan SEACREST

EASY

289/17	21/7	72/8	33/3	30/6	55/5	26/2
49/7	28/2	81/9	57/3	54/3	24/4	18/6
36/12	45/3	4/2	28/2	42/2	21/7	54/6
63/7	24/3	13/13	64/8	15/3	144/12	72/9
100/10	144/12	100/4	16/16	46/2	256/16	225/15
77/7	30/6	90/5	60/4	18/2	32/4	45/3
72/6	14/7	18/1	11/11	42/3	20/5	84/12

WORDS

1. terrell OWENS
2. salma HAYEK
3. marlon BRANDO
4. donnie MCCLURKIN

EASY

144/12	46/2	42/6	12/2	48/12	60/5	256/16
225/15	12/6	45/5	36/2	44/44	324/18	76/4
57/3	144/12	15/3	54/3	12/3	42/3	66/6
34/2	12/1	54/3	45/5	441/21	75/5	48/4
484/24	44/4	36/4	76/4	144/12	60/4	54/6
121/11	13/13	42/2	100/10	40/5	28/2	22/2
38/2	26/2	20/10	36/9	81/9	48/4	169/13

WORDS

1. ace HOOD
2. nate BERKUS
3. kirk FRANKLIN
4. venus WILLIAMS

EASY

169/13	15/3	24/3	441/21	256/16	42/3	48/3
42/3	34/17	255/15	38/2	10/2	324/18	45/9
75/3	25/5	36/3	56/8	15/3	676/26	36/2
52/2	441/21	15/3	40/5	39/3	5/1	625/25
144/12	16/4	45/3	5/5	42/6	60/12	76/4
72/6	64/8	90/18	100/10	24/6	42/2	49/7
36/6	14/2	45/3	75/5	484/24	32/4	625/25

WORDS

1. kevin JAMES
2. dl HUGHLEY
3. meagan GOOD
4. ellen DEGENERES

93

EASY

25/5	21/3	39/3	4/4	27/9	256/16	46/2
225/15	57/3	14/14	324/18	63/7	48/4	72/8
361/19	45/3	56/8	36/2	100/5	100/4	144/12
121/11	144/12	38/2	54/9	25/5	100/4	32/4
14/14	100/5	60/3	45/3	63/9	56/8	26/2
81/9	100/10	225/15	72/8	289/17	45/3	441/21
52/2	14/7	36/3	45/9	121/11	12/3	144/12

WORDS

1. michael MYERS
2. ray LIOTTA
3. nate DOGG
4. robin WILLIAMS

EASY

12/6	36/9	12/3	100/10	121/11	76/4	144/12
15/5	36/2	36/9	361/19	13/1	256/16	400/20
441/21	46/2	11/11	25/5	36/4	32/8	676/26
625/25	50/5	14/7	28/2	81/9	60/3	88/8
72/8	9/3	45/3	4/2	12/3	32/4	54/3
10/2	52/2	42/3	81/9	44/2	12/12	144/12
169/13	196/14	20/1	15/3	57/3	289/17	441/21

WORDS

1. jaden SMITH
2. quincy JONES
3. russell BRAND
4. lenny KRAVITZ

EASY

14/2	144/12	46/2	14/14	48/4	48/12	6/6
60/4	100/5	25/5	441/21	625/25	60/5	9/3
529/23	100/10	46/2	63/7	50/2	81/9	15/3
40/5	25/5	121/11	32/8	100/5	60/3	169/13
196/14	21/7	28/7	34/34	27/9	1/1	28/2
36/4	45/5	16/8	54/3	42/3	48/8	45/3
72/12	18/6	144/12	72/8	88/8	40/2	90/5

WORDS

1. jennifer l. HEWITT
2. wayne BRADY
3. bill CLINTON
4. ben WALLACE

EASY

76/4	144/12	25/5	81/9	100/10	121/11	196/14
18/9	39/3	19/1	35/5	15/3	45/9	441/21
12/12	400/20	529/23	35/7	48/4	75/3	45/3
64/8	144/12	18/9	15/15	42/3	54/3	55/11
60/5	39/3	40/5	42/3	100/10	45/3	54/3
46/2	45/3	18/6	676/26	625/25	50/5	36/2
25/5	26/2	75/5	12/3	21/7	4/4	55/5

WORDS

1. kevin MCHALE
2. nora JONES
3. jim CARREY
4. richard SMALLWOOD

EASY

225/15	256/16	441/21	15/15	42/3	15/3	18/3
42/3	42/6	32/4	484/24	625/25	324/18	72/8
15/3	24/4	256/16	40/2	225/15	28/2	76/4
144/12	6/2	42/3	14/14	42/2	30/6	40/5
25/5	35/7	11/11	36/2	36/3	10/5	84/7
21/3	24/6	54/3	12/4	81/9	45/3	60/5
60/4	48/12	44/4	56/8	441/21	15/15	21/7

WORDS

1. sanaa LATHAN
2. nancy GRACE
3. kirstie ALLEN
4. laurence FISHBURNE

EASY

√16	√49	√64	√81	√196	√100	√121
√196	√361	√144	√49	√225	√441	√400
√81	√1	√484	√4	√400	√196	√576
√16	√529	√16	√9	√225	√16	√81
√225	√16	√9	√196	√144	√400	√361
√676	√225	√256	√676	√625	√400	√49
√64	√49	√9	√324	√1	√81	√25

WORDS

1. barry BONDS
2. kyla PRATT
3. denzel WASHINGTON
4. cuba GOODING jr

EASY

√9	√441	√484	√529	√576	√81	√225
√225	√25	√121	√196	√256	√361	√196
√16	√49	√100	√9	√25	√324	√169
√400	√196	√25	√225	√25	√484	√25
√9	√1	√324	√256	√36	√64	√16
√676	√625	√256	√676	√441	√361	√196
√256	√81	√400	√484	√289	√1	√576

WORDS

1. chris ROCK
2. martin SHEEN
3. scottie PIPPEN
4. pamela ANDERSON

EASY

√169	√9	√16	√225	√196	√25	√144
√196	√100	√81	√196	√144	√1	√121
√324	√529	√144	√16	√361	√25	√144
√16	√9	√144	√1	√144	√16	√400
√676	√81	√625	√25	√576	√25	√100
√529	√400	√64	√441	√64	√484	√81
√121	√144	√225	√256	√9	√324	√361

WORDS

1. kate WINSLET
2. lauryn HILL
3. don CHEADLE
4. michael MCDONALD

EASY

√256	√100	√225	√25	√576	√529	√49
√289	√196	√441	√400	√324	√1	√225
√256	√25	√4	√81	√400	√361	√9
√361	√1	√169	√64	√36	√400	√64
√441	√100	√169	√81	√441	√81	√81
√625	√676	√49	√441	√1	√144	√196
√25	√36	√400	√361	√400	√25	√144

WORDS

1. pat SUMMIT
2. marion JONES
3. faith HILL
4. Brittany GASTINEAU

EASY

$\sqrt{121}$	$\sqrt{361}$	$\sqrt{1}$	$\sqrt{324}$	$\sqrt{441}$	$\sqrt{400}$	$\sqrt{484}$
$\sqrt{9}$	$\sqrt{49}$	$\sqrt{256}$	$\sqrt{196}$	$\sqrt{81}$	$\sqrt{169}$	$\sqrt{225}$
$\sqrt{441}$	$\sqrt{36}$	$\sqrt{25}$	$\sqrt{144}$	$\sqrt{64}$	$\sqrt{676}$	$\sqrt{400}$
$\sqrt{625}$	$\sqrt{81}$	$\sqrt{100}$	$\sqrt{324}$	$\sqrt{144}$	$\sqrt{121}$	$\sqrt{81}$
$\sqrt{25}$	$\sqrt{4}$	$\sqrt{169}$	$\sqrt{324}$	$\sqrt{25}$	$\sqrt{169}$	$\sqrt{196}$
$\sqrt{121}$	$\sqrt{225}$	$\sqrt{144}$	$\sqrt{441}$	$\sqrt{25}$	$\sqrt{4}$	$\sqrt{256}$
$\sqrt{49}$	$\sqrt{1}$	$\sqrt{144}$	$\sqrt{324}$	$\sqrt{196}$	$\sqrt{400}$	$\sqrt{121}$

WORDS

1. marissa MILLER
2. james BLUNT
3. jennifer GARNER
4. justin TIMBERLAKE

EASY

√81	√144	√16	√25	√9	√25	√361
√1	√100	√144	√121	√576	√196	√529
√441	√169	√81	√400	√256	√324	√225
√529	√361	√25	√529	√289	√100	√576
√676	√324	√400	√324	√625	√529	√225
√16	√9	√100	√1	√400	√225	√121
√144	√25	√1	√361	√9	√64	√16

WORDS

1. michelle WILLIAMS
2. january JONES
3. nick CARTER
4. clint EASTWOOD

EASY

√100	√121	√169	√361	√4	√9	√144
√169	√441	√1	√64	√484	√676	√400
√196	√625	√25	√16	√576	√324	√529
√576	√225	√196	√1	√441	√25	√676
√121	√361	√81	√9	√169	√361	√324
√49	√9	√169	√16	√81	√256	√676
√576	√324	√225	√16	√529	√289	√100

WORDS

1. donald TRUMP
2. taraji p. HENSON
3. rachel MCADAMS
4. andy RODDICK

EASY

√16	√4	√49	√100	√16	√121	√529
√144	√81	√441	√25	√121	√25	√64
√25	√196	√169	√289	√400	√81	√9
√4	√49	√225	√676	√36	√64	√1
√256	√25	√121	√225	√324	√441	√256
√484	√324	√81	√100	√25	√324	√676
√625	√529	√441	√400	√225	√81	√4

WORDS

1. betty WHITE
2. maya MOORE
3. justin BIEBER
4. leonardo DECAPRIO

EASY

$\sqrt{256}$	$\sqrt{400}$	$\sqrt{225}$	$\sqrt{324}$	$\sqrt{361}$	$\sqrt{49}$	$\sqrt{25}$
$\sqrt{64}$	$\sqrt{121}$	$\sqrt{81}$	$\sqrt{169}$	$\sqrt{81}$	$\sqrt{121}$	$\sqrt{196}$
$\sqrt{144}$	$\sqrt{441}$	$\sqrt{484}$	$\sqrt{324}$	$\sqrt{361}$	$\sqrt{9}$	$\sqrt{225}$
$\sqrt{400}$	$\sqrt{529}$	$\sqrt{324}$	$\sqrt{289}$	$\sqrt{400}$	$\sqrt{225}$	$\sqrt{25}$
$\sqrt{256}$	$\sqrt{25}$	$\sqrt{144}$	$\sqrt{25}$	$\sqrt{9}$	$\sqrt{324}$	$\sqrt{169}$
$\sqrt{196}$	$\sqrt{36}$	$\sqrt{100}$	$\sqrt{196}$	$\sqrt{529}$	$\sqrt{81}$	$\sqrt{64}$
$\sqrt{49}$	$\sqrt{81}$	$\sqrt{1}$	$\sqrt{64}$	$\sqrt{100}$	$\sqrt{361}$	$\sqrt{121}$

WORDS

1. will SMITH
2. jennifer LEWIS
3. lou FERRIGNO
4. herbie HANCOCK

EASY

√144	√121	√441	√400	√625	√676	√289
√529	√225	√16	√361	√25	√144	√1
√36	√256	√25	√49	√225	√100	√36
√49	√25	√121	√196	√144	√4	√196
√361	√64	√361	√400	√441	√169	√9
√400	√9	√441	√225	√361	√1	√25
√441	√196	√676	√64	√625	√529	√484

WORDS

1. lisa LOPES
2. george w. BUSH
3. laz ALONSO
4. morris CHESTNUT

EASY

√64	√289	√441	√196	√196	√225	√400
√25	√256	√225	√25	√1	√256	√196
√1	√625	√144	√484	√361	√25	√400
√441	√324	√484	√400	√196	√144	√400
√121	√144	√1	√324	√225	√25	√36
√9	√49	√1	√64	√9	√49	√81
√16	√256	√676	√361	√625	√289	√529

WORDS

1. keyshia COLE
2. john LENNON
3. kevin GARNETT
4. maria SHARAPOVA

EASY

√121	√1	√4	√9	√1	√400	√16
√676	√625	√1	√144	√25	√36	√64
√49	√9	√225	√529	√196	√324	√25
√121	√144	√625	√9	√1	√169	√324
√81	√1	√16	√49	√196	√289	√400
√169	√256	√81	√324	√361	√400	√441
√484	√9	√196	√121	√25	√49	√36

WORDS

1. james FRANCO
2. jack BLACK
3. jada PINKETT
4. floyd MAYWEATHER

110

EASY

$\sqrt{49}$	$\sqrt{121}$	$\sqrt{100}$	$\sqrt{196}$	$\sqrt{441}$	$\sqrt{676}$	$\sqrt{625}$
$\sqrt{25}$	$\sqrt{196}$	$\sqrt{225}$	$\sqrt{361}$	$\sqrt{324}$	$\sqrt{1}$	$\sqrt{169}$
$\sqrt{529}$	$\sqrt{400}$	$\sqrt{81}$	$\sqrt{400}$	$\sqrt{4}$	$\sqrt{16}$	$\sqrt{4}$
$\sqrt{16}$	$\sqrt{225}$	$\sqrt{9}$	$\sqrt{256}$	$\sqrt{25}$	$\sqrt{81}$	$\sqrt{676}$
$\sqrt{625}$	$\sqrt{324}$	$\sqrt{400}$	$\sqrt{361}$	$\sqrt{169}$	$\sqrt{64}$	$\sqrt{49}$
$\sqrt{361}$	$\sqrt{25}$	$\sqrt{289}$	$\sqrt{81}$	$\sqrt{25}$	$\sqrt{81}$	$\sqrt{361}$
$\sqrt{9}$	$\sqrt{256}$	$\sqrt{64}$	$\sqrt{256}$	$\sqrt{289}$	$\sqrt{324}$	$\sqrt{625}$

WORDS

1. leann RIMES
2. chris MARTIN
3. tyrese GIBSON
4. sherri SHEPHERD

EASY

√625	√144	√16	√361	√144	√441	√484
√400	√169	√1	√25	√169	√529	√400
√225	√400	√81	√144	√81	√121	√324
√144	√196	√196	√400	√144	√25	√9
√81	√49	√121	√64	√64	√676	√625
√529	√400	√441	√25	√144	√121	√1
√9	√16	√36	√484	√400	√400	√676

WORDS

1. alex SMITH
2. david GUETTA
3. sienna MILLER
4. andy DALTON

EASY

√121	√36	√441	√25	√324	√484	√100
√9	√81	√169	√36	√529	√289	√400
√441	√169	√361	√324	√25	√256	√324
√81	√529	√225	√361	√9	√324	√16
√361	√64	√225	√1	√81	√121	√196
√1	√169	√9	√49	√4	√25	√16
√4	√441	√361	√1	√484	√625	√676

WORDS

1. shemar MOORE
2. larry BIRD
3. andre AGASSI
4. david SCHWIMMER

EASY

√441	√100	√324	√400	√196	√25	√49
√81	√225	√361	√144	√196	√256	√144
√225	√196	√529	√225	√1	√81	√25
√441	√64	√484	√81	√256	√361	√529
√100	√225	√289	√361	√9	√144	√324
√361	√400	√441	√25	√81	√196	√36
√64	√289	√36	√324	√1	√144	√400

WORDS

1. gwyneth PALTROW
2. lisa LESLIE
3. magic JOHNSON
4. joe FRANCIS

EASY

√225	√529	√144	√441	√25	√49	√121
√225	√324	√169	√100	√484	√361	√529
√16	√361	√225	√1	√81	√256	√25
√4	√9	√196	√81	√169	√81	√625
√64	√81	√100	√144	√25	√144	√676
√484	√289	√144	√16	√289	√144	√25
√196	√9	√529	√81	√100	√1	√196

WORDS

1. brandy NORWOOD
2. patrick DEMPSEY
3. ray ALLEN
4. katt WILLIAMS

EASY

√289	√4	√25	√16	√324	√64	√121
√144	√441	√625	√676	√196	√225	√484
√64	√81	√225	√1	√529	√36	√100
√100	√196	√144	√64	√16	√4	√121
√625	√9	√144	√324	√400	√9	√361
√529	√100	√225	√196	√324	√25	√144
√121	√169	√196	√1	√4	√100	√441

WORDS

1. jonah HILL
2. michael JORDAN
3. tyson BECKFORD
4. carmelo ANTHONY

ANSWERS

PAGE 7

			11+2=M (4)		6+3=I (3)	
	5+3=H (2)	1+0=A (4)			14+8=V (3)	
	1+0=A (2)	14+4=R (4)	1+0=A (1)			3+2=E (3)
10+2=L (2)	3+0=C (4)			4+2=F (1)	15+3=R (3)	
	8+4=L (2)	6+2=H (4)	3+3=F (1)		10+9=S (3)	5+6=K (1)
			10+2=L (1)	11+4=O (3)	2+1=C (1)	
				4+1=E (1)	12+2=N (3)	

PAGE 8

	6+4=J (2)	7+2=I (4)			11+8=S (3)	
	1+0=A (2)	13+6=S (4)	6+6=L (4)	1+0=A (3)		
		2+1=C (2)	12+11=W (3)	3+2=E (4)	15+10=Y (4)	8+6=N (1)
		9+2=K (2)	13+12=Y (3)	3+1=D (1)	13+2=O (1)	
	14+5=S (2)		2+2=D (1)	4+1=E (3)		
11+4=O (2)			1+0=A (1)		15+3=R (3)	
	7+7=N (2)	5+3=H (1)				

12+4=P (4)		18+1=S (4)				
8+8=P (4)	1+0=A (4)			16+3=S (1)	8+7=O (1)	
	7+3=J (1)			8+3=K (1)		11+3=N (1)
		1+0=A (1)	2+1=C (1)		14+4=R (3)	
			5+2=G (2)	11+7=R (3)		4+1=E (3)
	3+0=C (2)	1+0=A (2)		4+1=E (2)		10+1=K (3)

			3+1=D (3)	15+3=R (3)		
		1+0=A (3)			1+0=A (3)	
	10+8=R (2)	15+8=W (3)	15+5=T (1)	12+8=T (1)		5+3=H (3)
	1+0=A (3)	4+1=E (2)	10+5=O (1)		7+5=L (4)	
17+8=Y (3)		2+1=C (1)	6+1=G (2)	3+2=E (4)		1+0=A (4)
		15+4=S (1)	4+3=G (2)	1+0=A (2)	6+4=J (2)	1+1=B (4)

		7+4=K (4)	2+1=C (4)		7+3=J (4)	
	12+7=S (4)			1+0=A (4)		
	13+2=O (4)		3+1=D (1)	3+2=E (1)		9+6=O (2)
9+5=N (4)		1+0=A (1)			7+5=L (2)	
	14+5=S (3)	20+3=W (1)		2+0=B (2)		
	15+3=R (3)			1+0=A (2)	11+5=P (2)	
	11+2=M (3)	1+0=A (3)				

			9+2=K (3)	4+1=E (3)		
	1+1=B (3)	1+0=A (3)			12+6=R (3)	
			7+7=N (1)	6+2=H (1)		
					14+1=O (1)	9+1=J (1)
	3+2=E (2)	8+6=N (4)	12+2=N (4)	14+5=S (2)		
	5+4=I (4)	10+6=P (2)	9+7=P (2)	1+0=A (4)		
5+2=G (4)	12+2=N (4)				4+2=F (4)	

				15+4=S (3)	11+4=O (4)		
	4+1=E (4)	12+2=N (4)	7+2=I (4)	13+5=R (4)	16+9=Y (3)		
2+2=D (4)			2+1=C (1)	6+5=K (1)		3+2=E (3)	
		5+4=I (1)				10+1=K (3)	
		11+11=V (1)					
		7+5=L (2)			13+3=P (2)		
			14+7=U (2)	1+0=A (2)			

		8+2=J (4)				
5+2=G (3)	1+0=A (4)		1+0=A (1)	11+9=T (1)		
2+1=C (4)	4+1=E (3)	16+4=T (1)			15+6=U (1)	
7+4=K (4)		15+3=R (3)	3+2=E (3)		7+6=M (1)	
11+8=S (4)	10+3=M (2)					
13+2=O (4)		11+4=O (2)		13+5=R (2)	4+1=E (2)	
	10+4=N (4)		8+7=O (2)			

121

				5+3=H (4)	8+1=I (4)	
14+2=P (2)				17+2=S (4)	1+1=B (1)	1+0=A (4)
	7+2=I (2)		1+0=A (4)		6+3=I (1)	13+1=N (4)
		16+4=T (2)	2+2=D (4)	16+2=R (1)		
	11+9=T (2)	11+7=R (4)		3+1=D (1)		
	1+0=A (4)				1+0=A (3)	
	7+4=K (4)	4+1=E (3)	6+6=L (3)	1+1=B (3)		

				2+1=C (3)		17+8=Y (4)
		2+0=B (2)	1+0=A (3)			12+3=O (4)
	1+0=A (2)		8+5=M (3)		7+7=N (2)	17+4=U (4)
	11+1=L (2)	10+6=P (3)		7+2=I (2)	12+2=N (4)	5+3=H (1)
	1+1=B (3)	3+1=D (2)	10+13=W (2)		6+1=G (4)	12+7=S (1)
	3+2=E (3)				1+0=A (1)	
10+2=L (3)	8+4=L (3)				3+1=D (1)	

122

		3+2=E (1)	11+4=O (3)	13+1=N (3)		16+2=R (4)
		10+10=T (3)	6+1=G (1)			4+1=E (4)
	16+4=T (3)		1+0=A (1)		15+3=R (4)	
13+3=P (3)	1+0=A (3)			2+1=C (1)	10+5=O (4)	17+2=S (2)
				10+12=V (2)	6+3=I (2)	2+2=D (4)
		2+2=D (2)	1+0=A (2)	4+2=F (4)	4+1=E (4)	

			6+1=G (2)	1+0=A (4)	18+4=V (4)	
		13+1=N (2)	9+5=N (4)			3+2=E (4)
	7+4=K (2)	7+2=I (2)	11+8=S (4)		10+9=S (1)	
			4+3=G (1)			
		2+1=C (3)	10+1=K (3)	5+2=G (1)		11+3=N (3)
	1+0=A (3)		7+2=I (1)	17+2=S (3)	13+2=O (3)	
9+1=J (3)			1+1=B (1)			

			4+2=F (4)			
				9+6=O (4)	13+13=Z (3)	
		18+7=Y (1)	12+12=X (4)	17+2=S (2)		4+1=E (3)
		7+5=L (1)	16+8=X (4)		2+0=B (2)	2+2=D (3)
	10+2=L (1)			1+1=B (2)		12+2=N (3)
	1+0=A (1)			12+3=O (2)		4+1=E (3)
16+3=S (1)			5+3=H (2)		7+6=M (3)	

			11+1=L (1)			
7+4=K (2)				3+2=E (1)	16+4=T (4)	
	3+2=E (2)			9+5=N (1)		15+3=R (4)
		14+0=N (2)	14+1=O (1)		1+0=A (4)	
		7+7=N (2)				6+2=H (4)
			4+1=E (2)	2+2=D (2)		
	5+2=G (3)	8+1=I (3)	6+6=L (3)	8+4=L (3)	20+5=Y (2)	

	5+1=F (4)	13+2=O (4)		1+0=A (2)		
			10+8=R (4)		5+4=I (2)	
	1+1=B (1)	1+0=A (1)		3+1=D (4)	9+2=K (2)	
			17+2=S (1)	11+8=S (1)		4+1=E (2)
	1+0=A (3)	6+2=H (3)			10+4=N (2)	
11+3=N (3)		13+2=O (3)	14+1=O (3)			
	15+4=S (3)	18+1=S (3)	5+5=J (3)	12+2=N (3)		

				16+2=R (2)		4+1=E (2)
		3+3=F (2)	3+2=E (2)		14+4=R (2)	11+1=L (2)
	11+5=P (4)	17+1=R (4)			7+5=L (2)	
		5+4=I (4)	3+1=D (1)	3+2=E (4)		
	10+13=W (3)		2+1=C (4)	1+0=A (1)	20+2=V (1)	7+2=I (1)
		4+1=E (3)				16+3=S (1)
	12+8=T (3)	15+4=S (3)				

15+8=W (2)			15+4=S (4)	1+0=A (1)		
	14+1=O (2)	7+6=M (4)		6+1=G (1)		
	1+1=B (2)	1+0=A (4)	5+4=I (4)		1+0=A (1)	
		4+1=E (2)		11+1=L (4)	5+2=G (1)	12+2=N (3)
		15+5=T (2)	6+6=L (4)		8+7=O (3)	1+0=A (3)
	18+5=W (4)	7+2=I (4)		9+1=J (3)	17+2=S (3)	

		6+6=L (4)	3+0=C (1)	4+1=E (4)		
	3+2=E (4)		1+1=B (4)	1+0=A (1)	7+2=I (4)	
15+3=R (4)		4+4=H (2)	8+7=O (2)	11+3=N (1)		9+2=K (4)
	12+8=T (2)		8+6=N (1)	9+4=M (2)		
			9+6=O (1)	11+3=N (3)	10+6=P (2)	
	15+6=U (3)	13+5=R (3)	1+0=A (3)	13+1=N (1)		11+8=S (2)
			1+1=B (3)	7+7=N (2)	12+3=O (2)	

				1+0=A (4)		
		11+4=O (2)	11+2=M (4)			
	11+1=L (4)	5+4=I (4)	12+2=N (2)	17+5=V (1)		15+4=S (1)
			3+2=E (1)	6+3=I (2)	5+0=E (1)	
	3+1=D (3)	1+0=A (3)	4+1=E (1)		2+1=C (2)	
	17+2=S (3)	14+4=R (1)			1+0=A (2)	
5+3=H (3)				14+2=P (2)		

	1+1=B (4)				8+8=P (3)	
1+0=A (4)		1+0=A (1)			1+0=A (3)	
7+4=K (4)	13+10=W (1)	10+8=R (2)	11+8=S (1)	6+2=H (1)	5+2=G (3)	
4+1=E (4)	15+3=R (4)		12+6=R (2)		7+2=I (1)	4+1=E (3)
	6+5=K (2)	4+1=E (2)		12+2=N (1)		
			8+6=N (1)		5+2=G (1)	
			11+4=O (1)	12+8=T (1)		

					2+1=C (4)		
15+3=R (4)		8+3=K (2)	14+7=U (2)		4+4=H (4)		
	4+1=E (4)	10+2=L (4)	10+4=N (2)	1+0=A (4)	17+2=S (1)		
		6+3=I (2)	3+1=D (4)	12+2=N (4)	3+2=E (1)	17+8=Y (3)	
		12+7=S (2)		8+6=N (1)		10+3=M (3)	
	1+1=B (3)	3+2=E (3)	6+6=L (3)	14+1=O (1)	1+0=A (3)		
			6+4=J (1)	9+3=L (3)			

		11+12=W (2)	9+7=P (3)	15+6=U (3)		
	1+0=A (2)		3+2=E (3)		1+0=A (3)	
	21+4=Y (2)	12+6=R (3)	7+7=N (4)	4+1=E (1)		7+5=L (3)
	1+0=A (2)	16+2=R (1)	3+2=E (1)	9+6=O (4)	11+2=M (1)	
7+7=N (2)	4+2=F (1)			15+3=R (4)	1+0=A (1)	
10+9=S (2)					4+1=E (4)	11+3=N (1)
				15+5=T (4)	5+3=H (4)	

128

	16+2=R (4)				11+8=S (2)	
		3+2=E (4)				4+1=E (2)
	22+3=Y (4)		17+3=T (1)			8+6=N (2)
	12+2=N (4)	3+2=E (1)	6+6=L (3)		8+7=O (2)	
10+5=O (4)		5+2=G (1)		17+4=U (3)	6+4=J (2)	
7+5=L (4)		15+4=S (4)	1+0=A (1)	3+1=D (3)		
	3+1=D (4)		10+9=S (1)		1+1=B (3)	1+0=A (3)

				12-10=B (3)		
			17-12=E (3)		50-25=Y (1)	
		15-5=J (2)	16-8=H (3)		17-2=O (1)	
	20-5=O (2)		25-24=A (3)	10-7=C (1)		
		28-14=N (2)	30-12=R (3)	6-3=C (1)		
	30-7=W (4)	7-2=E (2)	26-13=M (1)		12-7=E (4)	12-8=D (4)
	25-6=S (2)	12-11=A (4)	25-7=R (4)	14-7=G (4)		

	16-14=B (3)					
	13-12=A (3)		18-13=E (1)			18-12=F (4)
		20-0=T (3)		13-10=C (1)		25-10=O (4)
	20-7=M (2)		15-10=E (3)	25-6=S (3)	19-1=R (1)	30-12=R (4)
		17-14=C (2)		17-3=N (2)	15-10=E (1)	10-5=E (4)
		16-13=C (2)	27-18=I (2)	20-11=I (1)	16-2=N (4)	26-13=M (4)
			14-13=A (2)	30-14=P (1)	15-14=A (4)	

		30-11=S (1)	20-0=T (1)		75-50=Y (3)	
			10-9=A (1)	15-10=E (3)	27-9=R (2)	
	12-4=H (3)		44-22=V (3)	19-14=E (1)		10-5=E (2)
		14-13=A (3)	28-10=R (3)	20-18=B (1)	30-16=N (4)	16-8=H (2)
		22-11=K (2)	20-12=H (4)	42-28=N (4)	7-4=C (2)	17-2=O (4)
	12-2=J (4)	20-5=O (4)	42-21=U (2)	25-5=T (2)	20-1=S (4)	

	38-19=S (3)	14-9=E (3)		17-7=J (3)		
			16-2=N (3)	23-8=O (3)		20-17=C (2)
		20-14=F (1)	44-33=K (4)		11-10=A (2)	
12-4=H (4)	10-9=A (4)	24-10=N (4)	20-8=L (1)	25-6=S (4)	26-13=M (2)	
			17-16=A (1)		18-13=E (2)	
	25-10=O (1)		12-9=C (1)	42-28=N (2)		36-18=R (2)
		13-10=C (1)			45-30=O (2)	

PAGE 34

		27-12=O (2)	15-5=J (2)			
	42-28=N (2)			20-7=M (3)	25-10=O (3)	
	25-24=A (2)		12-7=E (3)			25-5=T (3)
		27-8=S (2)	18-9=I (3)	48-32=P (1)		
				30-14=P (1)		
			20-11=I (4)	24-4=T (4)	10-5=E (1)	
	46-23=W (4)	16-8=H (4)		7-2=E (4)	16-12=D (1)	

		30-12=R (1)		12-6=F (4)	36-18=R (2)		
		12-7=E (1)		15-14=A (4)	35-30=E (2)		
			21-14=G (1)	30-9=U (4)		44-33=K (2)	
			15-10=E (1)		13-10=C (4)	11-10=A (2)	
	24-10=N (3)	29-10=S (1)		19-14=E (4)	12-10=B (2)		
		30-7=W (3)	14-13=A (3)	17-9=H (3)	27-7=T (4)		

	30-16=N (4)		30-18=L (4)		54-36=R (1)		
15-10=E (4)		10-9=A (4)		17-12=E (1)			
		18-10=H (2)		26-13=M (1)			
	23-22=A (2)				24-12=L (1)		
	15-2=M (2)				16-15=A (1)	25-20=E (3)	
		30-17=M (2)		30-14=P (1)		18-9=I (3)	
			17-7=J (3)	45-30=O (3)	36-24=L (3)		

	20-18=B (3)					
		30-21=I (3)		24-12=L (4)		16-8=H (1)
		14-10=D (3)		18-13=E (4)	30-11=S (1)	
	15-10=E (3)		18-14=D (4)		14-13=A (1)	
	30-16=N (3)	12-8=D (2)	24-10=N (4)	25-11=N (1)		
		14-13=A (4)	20-11=I (2)		26-8=R (2)	
		26-13=M (4)		15-10=E (2)		

		18-12=F (4)	48-36=L (4)	15-14=A (4)	30-8=V (4)	
			17-3=N (1)	45-30=O (1)		
	18-14=D (3)				38-19=S (1)	
		17-12=E (3)			30-10=T (1)	
		11-10=A (3)		10-9=A (1)		75-50=Y (2)
	30-17=M (2)		20-6=N (3)	46-23=W (1)	17-12=E (2)	
		14-13=A (2)	25-7=R (2)	36-24=L (2)		

17-7=J (4)			66-55=K (3)			
60-45=O (4)			45-30=O (3)		26-7=S (1)	
24-16=H (4)	14-11=C (2)		17-13=D (3)		44-33=K (1)	
20-6=N (4)		11-10=A (2)		20-10=J (3)		28-14=N (1)
	25-6=S (4)	30-12=R (2)		30-15=O (3)	17-16=A (1)	
	16-1=O (4)		40-20=T (2)	15-10=E (3)	12-10=B (1)	
	14-0=N (4)		15-10=E (2)	28-10=R (2)		

PAGE 40

				36-18=R (3)		10-5=E (3)
	38-19=S (4)	12-6=F (3)	11-10=A (3)	20-16=D (1)	28-10=R (3)	24-12=L (3)
		17-12=E (4)	30-18=L (4)		30-12=R (1)	20-8=L (3)
			42-35=G (2)	33-10=W (4)	20-5=O (1)	
	33-22=K (4)	24-10=N (4)	45-30=O (4)	30-16=N (2)		15-9=F (1)
		22-11=K (2)	27-18=I (2)			

16-12=D (4)				30-17=M (3)	·	24-16=H (3)
	14-13=A (4)	30-12=R (3)	17-12=E (3)		39-26=M (3)	16-15=A (3)
	44-22=V (4)					
	17-8=I (4)		18-9=I (1)	25-11=N (1)		26-13=M (2)
	12-8=D (4)	36-24=L (1)				30-15=O (2)
	25-6=S (4)	18-17=A (1)	17-3=N (4)		22-18=D (2)	
	32-16=P (1)	17-2=O (4)		45-30=O (2)		

		13-10=C (2)	15-10=E (2)			42-35=G (4)
		36-18=R (3)	28-14=N (2)		26-12=N (1)	25-11=N (4)
		14-13=A (2)	11-6=E (3)	48-32=P (3)	17-2=O (1)	27-18=I (4)
			25-7=R (3)		30-11=S (1)	30-16=N (4)
	12-4=H (3)	17-16=A (3)		75-50=Y (1)	42-28=N (4)	
			25-5=T (1)	15-14=A (4)	20-7=M (4)	

						15-5=J (4)
			30-11=S (1)			45-30=O (4)
	25-6=S (2)		18-9=I (1)		32-24=H (4)	
		11-2=I (2)		36-18=R (1)		30-16=N (4)
		46-23=W (2)		28-10=R (1)	21-14=G (3)	38-19=S (4)
	18-13=E (2)		27-18=I (3)	16-2=N (3)	45-30=O (1)	30-15=O (4)
	30-18=L (2)		33-22=K (3)		24-10=N (1)	25-11=N (4)

		30-14=P (1)	15-1=N (4)		66-55=K (1)	
		60-45=O (4)	11-10=A (1)	30-12=R (1)		28-14=N (2)
	17-9=H (3)		29-10=S (4)			45-30=O (2)
		24-5=S (3)	25-23=B (4)		23-10=M (2)	
	14-13=A (3)	22-13=I (4)	14-10=D (2)	18-17=A (2)		
	14-11=C (3)		28-21=G (4)			

		30-5=Y (2)			18-13=E (4)	
		25-7=R (2)		23-9=N (1)		30-18=L (4)
			30-12=R (2)	20-11=I (1)	36-24=L (4)	
		15-10=E (2)		26-21=E (4)	22-21=A (1)	
	30-14=P (2)		25-23=B (4)		23-0=W (1)	
	24-12=L (4)	12-11=A (4)		27-7=T (1)		11-10=A (3)
		17-11=F (3)	30-15=O (3)	22-8=N (3)	15-11=D (3)	

		14-11=C (2)			32-24=H (4)	
		27-26=A (2)		25-24=A (4)		32-16=P (1)
	30-12=R (2)			26-13=M (4)		25-10=O (1)
	36-18=R (2)		44-33=K (1)	39-26=M (4)	23-11=L (1)	
			45-30=O (4)	26-25=A (1)	48-36=L (1)	
	14-12=B (3)	24-12=L (3)		42-28=N (4)	19-15=D (4)	
			18-9=I (3)	28-21=G (3)	15-10=E (3)	

						19-14=E (3)
	20-2=R (2)		29-10=S (1)		25-7=R (3)	
	15-10=E (2)		32-24=H (1)		60-45=O (3)	
40-20=T (4)	60-45=O (4)	34-23=K (2)		28-23=E (1)		30-17=M (3)
24-10=N (4)	30-7=W (2)	11-10=A (2)	24-12=L (2)	29-24=E (1)		100-75=Y (3)
	27-18=I (4)		42-28=N (1)		36-18=R (3)	
48-32=P (4)		18-16=B (3)	10-9=A (3)	30-12=R (3)		

		25-6=S (4)	30-18=L (2)			
			30-12=R (4)	17-12=E (2)		
25-10=O (1)		16-11=E (4)		46-23=W (2)		30-16=N (3)
	13-11=B (1)	17-13=D (4)		16-7=I (2)		24-23=A (3)
	16-15=A (1)		42-28=N (4)		38-19=S (2)	32-24=H (3)
		20-7=M (1)	12-11=A (4)		25-14=K (3)	
	12-11=A (1)			30-11=S (4)		

		42-21=U (4)		30-10=T (1)	
	16-2=N (4)		20-19=A (1)		14-9=E (1)
	17-13=D (4)	30-14=P (1)		36-24=L (1)	
		15-10=E (4)		24-10=N (3)	26-25=A (3)
	14-7=G (2)	20-2=R (4)	13-2=K (2)		24-16=H (3)
	33-10=W (4)	28-14=N (2)	15-6=I (2)	13-10=C (3)	
	45-30=O (4)	75-60=O (4)	4-0=D (4)		

	16-14=B (4)	17-7=J (3)		42-28=N (3)		38-19=S (3)
	14-13=A (4)		45-30=O (3)	26-8=R (1)	17-16=A (3)	
	14-11=C (2)	30-12=R (4)		30-15=O (1)		
		32-24=H (2)	55-44=K (4)		24-12=L (1)	
		10-5=E (2)		36-24=L (4)	75-50=Y (1)	
	19-0=S (2)		25-20=E (2)	16-15=A (1)	56-51=E (4)	
		16-2=N (2)	25-5=T (1)	26-1=Y (2)		30-5=Y (4)

				45-30=O (1)		
			40-20=T (1)		30-16=N (1)	30-11=S (2)
			10-9=A (1)		25-5=T (4)	24-10=N (2)
		11-6=E (1)			15-10=E (2)	45-25=T (4)
	34-23=K (1)				30-8=V (2)	60-45=O (4)
			21-14=G (2)	20-11=I (2)		13-10=C (4)
25-6=S (3)	44-33=K (3)	23-9=N (3)	14-13=A (3)	13-11=B (3)		29-10=S (4)

			18-0=R (2)			
		5-0=E (2)		18-0=R (2)	14-0=N (4)	
	16-0=P (2)			25-0=Y (2)	4-0=D (1)	15-0=O (4)
	19-0=S (3)			9-0=I (1)		19-0=S (4)
		5-0=E (3)		5-0=E (1)	14-0=N (4)	
	12-0=L (3)	11-0=K (3)	18-0=R (1)			1-0=A (4)
		5-0=E (3)	1-0=A (3)			13-0=M (4)

PAGE 53

	3X6=R (3)		2X7=N (3)	3X1=C (1)		
	3X5=O (3)	1X1=A (3)	3X5=O (1)	2X2=D (3)		
23X1=W (3)	3X4=L (3)		19X1=S (1)			
				2X1=B (1)	1X1=A (4)	2X7=N (2)
	2X6=L (2)		5X5=Y (1)		3X5=O (2)	2X10=T (4)
		3X5=O (2)	1X1=A (4)	2X2=D (2)		3X4=L (4)
	4X5=T (4)	2X9=R (4)	2X7=N (2)	2X11=V (4)	3X5=O (4)	

PAGE 54

			5X1=E (4)	2X7=N (4)		
		4X2=H (3)	2X6=L (4)		2X9=R (2)	
	1X1=A (3)		19X1=S (4)	5X1=E (1)		5X1=E (2)
	4X5=T (3)		3X5=O (4)	3X4=L (1)		4X5=T (2)
4X2=H (3)			3X5=O (1)	2X7=N (4)	2X9=R (2)	
	1X1=A (3)	3X1=C (1)	5X5=Y (3)		3X5=O (2)	
	23X1=W (3)	1X1=A (3)		2X8=P (2)		

PAGE 55

					2X7=N (1)	
3X6=R (2)				3X5=O (1)		
	3X5=O (2)			4X5=T (1)		
		19X1=S (2)	23X1=W (1)	2X10=T (4)	3X3=I (4)	
		19X1=S (2)	1X1=A (4)	5X1=E (1)		3X2=F (4)
	2X2=D (3)		4X3=L (4)	2X7=N (1)	3X3=I (3)	1X1=A (4)
		3X7=U (3)	4X4=P (3)	3X6=R (3)	2X4=H (4)	

PAGE 56

	2X7=N (4)	5X1=E (4)	2X7=N (3)			
	2X4=H (4)	1X1=A (3)				
3X1=C (4)		13X1=M (3)	3X5=O (1)	19X1=S (1)	2X2=D (2)	
	2X2=D (4)	13X1=M (1)	2X2=D (3)	2X9=R (2)	5X1=E (1)	
	2X7=N (4)		1X1=A (2)	3X5=O (3)	5X1=E (1)	
		3X7=U (4)	23X1=W (2)	3X5=O (3)		2X7=N (1)
	2X4=H (2)	3X5=O (2)	2X1=B (4)	7X1=G (3)		

	2X10=T (4)	4X4=P (3)		2X10=T (1)	3X5=O (1)	2X7=N (1)
		1X1=A (4)	3X5=O (3)	2X6=L (1)		
	2X1=B (2)	3X7=U (4)	5X1=E (3)		3X3=I (1)	
	2X9=R (4)	5X5=Y (2)	2X4=H (3)	5X1=E (3)	2X4=H (1)	
	1X1=A (4)	2X7=N (2)	3X4=L (3)		3X6=R (3)	
19X1=S (4)			5X1=E (2)			
	3X3=I (4)		19X1=S (2)			

	4X4=P (2)	3X6=R (2)				2X9=R (1)
	1X1=A (4)	19X1=S (4)	5X5=Y (2)		5X1=E (1)	
3X4=L (4)	3X6=R (2)	3X5=O (2)		4X5=T (1)		
3X7=U (4)	7X1=G (4)		3X4=L (1)	2X1=B (3)		
3X5=O (4)	2X2=D (4)		3X5=O (3)	1X1=A (1)	3X5=O (3)	
		3X4=L (3)		23X1=W (1)		

			2X9=R (2)	1X1=A (2)		
		7X1=G (2)		2X7=N (2)		
	2X10=T (4)	19X1=S (3)	4X5=T (2)		19X1=S (1)	
	5X1=E (3)	2X4=H (4)	2X2=D (3)	13X1=M (1)		
	2X2=D (3)	3X7=U (4)	3X6=R (3)		1X1=A (1)	
2X7=N (4)	2X9=R (4)	23X1=W (3)	1X1=A (3)		2X2=D (1)	
	1X1=A (4)	13X1=M (4)				1X1=A (1)

	3X1=C (3)	3X5=O (3)	3X5=O (3)		2X4=H (2)	
		3X6=R (1)	4X4=P (3)	5X1=E (3)	3X3=I (2)	
		3X5=O (1)		3X4=L (2)	2X9=R (3)	
		3X6=R (4)	2X1=B (1)	5X1=E (1)	19X1=S (2)	
	3X2=F (4)		5X1=E (4)		2X9=R (1)	3X5=O (2)
2X7=N (4)		5X5=Y (4)			4X5=T (1)	2X7=N (2)
	3X3=I (4)	23X1=W (4)		19X1=S (1)		

144

					2X7=N (4)	
	19X1=S (2)				2X2=D (1)	3X3=I (4)
	3X5=O (2)	23X1=W (2)	5X5=Y (3)	3X3=I (1)	3X2=F (4)	
3X5=O (2)			2X4=H (3)	3X4=L (1)	2X2=D (1)	3X2=F (4)
	2X8=P (2)		2X6=L (1)	4X4=P (3)	3X6=R (1)	3X3=I (4)
	19X1=S (2)	3X7=U (3)	3X6=R (3)	1X1=A (1)		2X9=R (4)
			13X1=M (3)			7X1=G (4)

19X1=S (1)			4X5=T (3)	3X4=L (2)		
	4X5=T (1)	2X10=T (3)			3X5=O (2)	
	3X7=U (1)	5X1=E (3)	2X2=D (1)	1X1=A (1)	4X4=P (2)	
	19X1=S (3)	2X2=D (1)	5X1=E (4)		3X6=R (1)	5X1=E (2)
	19X1=S (3)	3X4=L (4)	2X6=L (4)	23X1=W (4)	2X2=D (1)	13X2=Z (2)
		1X1=A (3)		3X5=O (4)		
			2X1=B (3)		3X1=C (4)	

		3X5=O (3)	2X2=D (3)				
	7X1=G (3)					13X1=M (2)	
	7X1=G (3)		1X1=A (1)	2X8=P (1)			3X3=I (2)
		3X3=I (1)					3X1=C (2)
	2X9=R (1)	2X7=N (1)				2X4=H (2)	
	3X5=O (4)	5X1=E (1)	4X5=T (1)	3X3=I (4)		5X1=E (2)	5X1=E (2)
2X7=N (4)		19X1=S (4)	3X4=L (4)	23X1=W (4)			12X1=L (2)

	19X1=S (4)		2X2=D (3)	3X6=R (3)	3X3=I (3)		
		2X8=P (4)	5X1=E (4)		5X5=Y (1)	22X1=V (3)	
	2X1=B (2)	3X6=R (4)	1X1=A (4)	2X9=R (1)		5X1=E (3)	
	19X1=S (4)	5X1=E (2)		23X1=W (1)	2X9=R (3)		
		2X7=N (2)			3X5=O (1)		
	2X7=N (2)				13X1=M (1)		
4X5=T (2)	2X10=T (2)	5X1=E (2)					

146

	2X2=D (4)			1X1=A (3)		
2X7=N (4)		19X1=S (1)		3X4=L (3)		
	1X1=A (4)		3X7=U (1)		2X1=B (3)	3X6=R (1)
	2X6=L (4)		13X1=M (1)	1X1=A (3)	5X1=E (1)	19X1=S (1)
	2X9=R (2)	5X1=E (4)		13X1=M (1)		
		3X5=O (2)	4X4=P (4)	3X5=O (4)		
		5X1=E (2)	19X1=S (2)		3X1=C (4)	

		5X1=E (2)	2X7=N (2)			
	3X1=C (1)		2X6=L (2)	3X4=L (2)		
	3X5=O (1)				1X1=A (2)	23X1=W (4)
15X1=O (1)			2X1=B (4)	3X4=L (4)	2X4=H (4)	1X1=A (4)
	11X1=K (1)		5X1=E (4)			2X10=T (3)
				2X9=R (4)	5X5=Y (3)	2X7=N (3)
			7X1=G (4)		19X1=S (3)	3X5=O (3)

			1X1=A (3)		13X1=M (1)	
		3X6=R (3)		2X6=L (4)	3X7=U (1)	
	2X4=H (2)	13X1=M (3)	5X1=E (4)	2X9=R (1)	3X4=L (4)	7X1=G (3)
	3X7=U (2)	3X6=R (4)	19X1=S (3)	4X4=P (1)	2X7=N (3)	5X5=Y (1)
	2X9=R (4)	2X2=D (2)	2X10=T (3)	3X5=O (3)	2X4=H (1)	
3X7=U (4)		19X1=S (2)	2X9=R (3)			
	2X1=B (4)		3X5=O (2)	2X7=N (2)		

	19X1=S (4)		3X1=C (3)			
	2X8=P (4)		3X5=O (3)			
	3X3=I (4)			3X5=O (3)	1X1=A (2)	
5X1=E (4)		2X4=H (1)	5X1=E (3)	4X4=P (3)	3X4=L (2)	
2X6=L (4)		2X9=R (3)	19X1=S (1)			2X6=L (2)
	2X1=B (4)	5X1=E (4)	3X7=U (1)			5X1=E (2)
		2X1=B (1)	3X6=R (4)	7X1=G (4)	2X7=N (2)	

19X1=S (1)			3X1=C (3)			2X6=L (4)
	23X1=W (1)		2X4=H (3)		13X1=M (2)	5X1=E (4)
		3X3=I (1)		1X1=A (3)	3X5=O (2)	4X5=T (4)
		3X2=F (1)		4X4=P (3)	2X10=T (4)	3X5=O (2)
			4X5=T (1)	3X4=L (3)	5X1=E (4)	2X9=R (2)
		2X7=N (3)	3X3=I (3)	3X6=R (4)	5X1=E (2)	
		2X7=N (4)	1X1=A (4)	13X1=M (4)		

		8X2=P (4)		5X1=E (3)		
19X1=S (2)		3X5=O (4)			2X6=L (3)	
	1X1=A (2)		3X6=R (4)	2X2=D (1)		3X4=L (3)
		2X7=N (2)	2X10=T (4)	1X1=A (1)		3X3=I (3)
		2X2=D (2)	2X11=V (1)	13X1=M (4)	3X5=O (3)	
	3X4=L (2)		1X1=A (4)	3X3=I (1)	2X10=T (3)	
	5X1=E (2)	3X6=R (2)	19X1=S (1)	2X7=N (4)		4X5=T (3)

	2X4=H (2)	3X4=L (4)	5X1=E (4)			
	2X8=P (4)	3X3=I (2)	2X6=L (2)	7X1=G (4)	1X1=A (4)	
4X4=P (4)				4X5=T (2)	3X5=O (2)	4X5=T (4)
	1X1=A (4)		5X1=E (1)		2X7=N (2)	5X1=E (4)
				19X1=S (1)		
	2X1=B (3)			3X5=O (1)	5X1=E (3)	
		3X7=U (3)	2X1=B (3)	2X6=L (3)	3X6=R (1)	

			2X7=N (4)			
2X7=N (2)				3X5=O (4)	3X6=R (3)	
	2X6=L (2)	1X1=A (1)	2X7=N (1)	19X1=S (4)	5X1=E (3)	1X1=A (1)
	19X1=S (1)	3X5=O (2)	3X3=I (4)	4X5=T (1)	2X7=N (1)	11X1=K (3)
		3X1=C (2)	3X6=R (4)	1X1=A (1)		2X9=R (3)
			2X7=N (2)	2X9=R (4)	3X5=O (4)	1X1=A (3)
		2X6=L (2)	3X3=I (2)		4X4=P (3)	13X1=M (4)

				1X1=A (3)			
	13X1=M (2)	3X7=U (2)		3X2=F (3)			
			2X9=R (2)	3X2=F (3)	5X1=E (1)		
		3X6=R (4)	4X4=P (2)	3X4=L (3)	2X10=T (1)		
		2X4=H (2)	5X1=E (4)	3X3=I (1)	5X1=E (3)		
		5X5=Y (2)	2X8=P (4)	2X4=H (1)	3X1=C (3)		
3X1=C (4)	3X5=O (4)	3X5=O (4)	23X1=W (1)				11X1=K (3)

			2X1=B (1)			
		3X4=L (3)		3X6=R (1)		
		5X1=E (3)	5X1=E (4)	3X5=O (1)		
	19X1=S (2)	2X11=V (3)	2X7=N (4)	23X1=W (1)		3X5=O (4)
	5X1=E (3)	4X4=P (2)	3X6=R (4)		2X7=N (1)	19X1=S (4)
	2X9=R (3)	1X1=A (2)		3X7=U (4)		2X1=B (4)
4X5=T (3)			2X2=D (2)	5X1=E (2)	3X5=O (4)	

	2X2=D (3)	3X3=I (3)		2X6=L (3)		
			5X1=E (3)		5X1=E (3)	4X4=P (1)
		3X6=R (1)		19X1=S (3)	1X1=A (1)	
3X4=L (4)			5X1=E (1)		2X9=R (1)	
	1X1=A (4)	2X7=N (4)		11X1=K (1)	5X5=Y (2)	
23X1=W (4)	13X1=M (2)	5X1=E (4)	3X1=C (4)	2X9=R (2)		
	2X9=R (4)	3X5=O (2)	23X1=W (2)	5X1=E (4)		

	12/12=A (3)					
		20/5=D (3)		20/10=B (4)		25/5=E (2)
	32/32=A (3)	57/3=S (1)	22/11=B (4)		44/2=V (2)	
	39/3=M (3)	12/12=A (4)	40/2=T (1)	44/44=A (2)		
76/4=S (3)		28/2=N (4)	72/8=I (1)	42/3=N (2)		
	9/3=C (4)	60/5=L (1)	38/2=S (2)		54/3=R (1)	
	26/2=M (4)		36/3=L (1)	30/6=E (1)		

		44/4=K (1)	36/2=R (2)			75/3=Y (3)
	38/2=S (1)	25/5=E (2)	54/3=R (1)			35/7=E (3)
		72/6=L (2)	14/14=A (1)		42/3=N (3)	
	48/4=L (2)	28/2=N (4)	76/4=S (4)	48/3=P (1)	30/2=O (3)	
	54/6=I (2)	34/34=A (4)	42/3=N (4)	38/2=S (1)		45/3=O (3)
26/2=M (2)			36/4=I (4)		24/2=L (3)	
		46/2=W (4)		12/4=C (3)		

		46/2=W (3)		28/7=D (3)		
	28/2=N (3)		45/3=O (3)			57/3=S (4)
	55/11=E (3)		45/9=E (1)		54/3=R (2)	39/3=M (4)
100/4=Y (3)		42/3=N (1)			11/11=A (4)	42/2=U (2)
			75/5=O (1)	63/7=I (4)	16/4=D (2)	
		45/5=I (4)	60/3=T (1)	60/5=L (4)	32/8=D (2)	
	46/2=W (4)	19/1=S (1)	84/7=L (4)			

		75/5=O (3)	60/3=T (3)	48/4=L (4)	36/3=L (4)	
	28/2=N (3)	39/3=M (2)	81/9=I (4)	48/2=X (3)		
		72/8=I (2)	32/4=H (4)	33/33=A (3)	76/4=S (1)	
	28/2=N (2)	15/5=C (4)		46/2=W (1)	36/2=R (3)	12/6=B (3)
	45/3=O (2)		36/2=R (4)	14/14=A (1)		
54/3=R (2)			42/2=U (4)		42/3=N (1)	
	12/4=C (4)	64/8=H (4)		44/4=K (1)		

PAGE 80

	42/3=N (3)			75/5=O (2)	9/3=C (2)	42/3=N (4)
		45/3=O (3)	60/5=L (2)		45/3=O (4)	55/5=K (2)
		36/3=L (2)	76/4=S (3)	13/13=A (1)		38/2=S (4)
		42/2=U (2)	54/6=I (3)		39/3=M (1)	42/3=N (4)
	22/11=B (2)	16/4=D (3)			14/14=A (1)	32/4=H (4)
	11/11=A (3)			16/8=B (1)	30/2=O (4)	
26/2=M (3)				45/3=O (1)		100/10=J (4)

					76/4=S (1)	
				35/7=E (1)		52/2=Z (3)
	28/2=N (2)		42/3=N (1)		20/4=E (3)	
	60/4=O (2)	63/7=I (4)	45/3=O (1)		39/3=M (3)	
	60/3=T (2)	32/32=A (4)	28/2=N (4)	50/5=J (1)		30/2=O (3)
	46/2=W (4)	75/3=Y (2)	34/34=A (2)			42/6=G (3)
40/2=T (4)				48/3=P (2)		

				28/2=N (4)	30/2=O (4)	72/8=I (4)	42/2=U (4)
	12/12=A (1)	81/9=I (1)	20/5=D (3)		80/4=T (2)	42/3=N (4)	
26/2=M (1)		24/2=L (1)		54/3=R (3)	42/3=N (2)		
	57/3=S (1)		48/4=L (1)		8/8=A (3)	32/32=A (2)	
			54/6=I (1)	25/5=E (3)		75/3=Y (2)	
		46/2=W (1)		32/4=H (3)	54/3=R (2)		
			38/2=S (3)		14/7=B (2)		

42/3=N (2)				13/13=A (3)		46/2=W (4)
35/7=E (2)				36/2=R (3)	54/3=R (1)	81/9=I (4)
	46/2=W (2)		20/1=T (3)	45/3=O (1)	54/6=I (4)	72/6=L (4)
	60/3=T (2)		21/7=C (3)	39/3=M (1)	48/4=L (4)	27/27=A (4)
		60/4=O (2)	25/5=E (3)		30/2=O (1)	26/2=M (4)
		42/3=N (2)		144/12=L (3)	15/3=E (3)	57/3=S (4)

		45/3=O (4)	12/4=C (3)	12/12=A (3)	39/3=M (3)	
	28/2=N (4)	40/2=T (4)			28/2=N (1)	48/3=P (3)
32/4=H (2)			76/4=S (4)	45/3=O (1)		24/12=B (3)
	60/4=O (2)		38/2=S (1)	49/7=G (4)		25/5=E (3)
		42/2=U (2)	36/3=L (1)	42/3=N (4)	60/5=L (3)	
		42/6=G (2)	36/4=I (4)	27/3=I (1)		48/4=L (3)
	32/4=H (2)		66/6=K (4)	46/2=W (1)		

			38/2=S (2)	45/3=O (2)	28/2=N (4)	
	42/6=G (4)	54/3=R (4)	42/3=N (1)	40/8=E (4)	26/2=M (2)	15/3=E (4)
		13/13=A (1)	25/5=E (4)		23/23=A (2)	
		39/3=M (1)	54/3=R (3)	14/14=A (3)		40/2=T (2)
	24/6=D (1)	16/8=B (3)			26/2=M (3)	57/3=S (2)
54/6=I (1)	11/11=A (3)				19/1=S (3)	
44/4=K (1)						

					18/6=C (3)	
	10/5=B (2)			30/2=O (3)		
28/2=N (4)		36/2=R (2)		60/4=O (3)		
26/26=A (4)		17/17=A (2)	77/7=K (3)			66/6=K (1)
39/3=M (4)	20/5=D (2)				15/5=C (1)	
	42/7=F (4)	75/3=Y (2)		72/8=I (1)		
		20/4=E (4)	32/4=H (4)	12/3=D (1)		

76/4=S (2)				42/3=N (1)		18/3=F (4)
	20/4=E (2)		36/4=I (1)		36/2=R (4)	
		39/3=M (2)	44/2=V (1)		20/20=A (4)	28/2=N (4)
	14/14=A (2)			35/7=E (1)	44/4=K (4)	38/2=S (3)
	60/6=J (2)			60/5=L (1)	32/2=P (3)	48/4=L (4)
			45/9=E (3)	48/3=P (3)	72/8=I (4)	28/2=N (4)

			28/2=N (3)			
38/2=S (4)		57/3=S (1)		14/14=A (3)	56/8=G (2)	64/8=H (2)
	28/7=D (4)		25/5=E (1)	21/7=C (3)	63/7=I (2)	80/4=T (2)
	36/3=L (4)		26/2=M (1)	42/3=N (2)	28/2=N (3)	
		45/9=E (4)	66/6=K (2)	144/12=L (1)		42/2=U (3)
	26/2=M (2)	12/4=C (2)	72/8=I (4)	75/5=O (1)		16/4=D (3)
			32/4=H (1)	40/5=H (4)	76/4=S (4)	

	38/2=S (4)	39/3=M (4)				
			2/2=A (4)	38/2=S (3)		
	34/34=A (2)	15/3=E (1)	18/2=I (4)	44/4=K (3)	60/3=T (1)	38/2=S (1)
	36/2=R (2)	24/2=L (4)	42/3=N (1)	30/2=O (1)	75/5=O (3)	
	44/2=V (2)	25/5=E (2)	60/5=L (4)			60/4=O (3)
	54/6=I (2)	27/3=I (4)				36/2=R (3)
54/3=R (2)	46/2=W (4)					12/6=B (3)

48/6=H (2)				45/9=E (4)	54/3=R (4)	46/2=W (1)
	30/2=O (2)		76/4=S (4)		45/5=I (1)	18/6=C (4)
		54/9=F (2)		60/3=T (4)	48/4=L (1)	22/22=A (4)
		57/3=S (1)	48/8=F (2)	24/2=L (1)		20/4=E (4)
	12/3=D (3)		81/9=I (1)	26/2=M (2)		38/2=S (4)
		27/3=I (3)	56/8=G (3)	3/3=A (2)		
			42/3=N (2)	63/9=G (3)	38/2=S (3)	

		72/8=I (4)	33/3=K (4)			26/2=M (4)
	28/2=N (4)		57/3=S (1)	54/3=R (4)		18/6=C (4)
			28/2=N (1)	42/2=U (4)	21/7=C (4)	
	24/3=H (2)	13/13=A (2)		15/3=E (1)	144/12=L (4)	
		100/4=Y (2)		46/2=W (1)		
77/7=K (2)	30/6=E (2)		60/4=O (1)			45/3=O (3)
	14/7=B (3)	18/1=R (3)	11/11=A (3)	42/3=N (3)	20/5=D (3)	

	46/2=W (4)		12/2=F (3)			
	12/6=B (2)	45/5=I (4)	36/2=R (3)	44/44=A (3)		
	144/12=L (4)	15/3=E (2)		12/3=D (1)	42/3=N (3)	66/6=K (3)
	12/1=L (4)	54/3=R (2)			75/5=O (1)	48/4=L (3)
	44/4=K (2)	36/4=I (4)	76/4=S (2)		60/4=O (1)	54/6=I (3)
	13/13=A (4)	42/2=U (2)		40/5=H (1)	28/2=N (3)	
38/2=S (4)	26/2=M (4)					

						42/3=N (4)	
			38/2=S (1)	10/2=E (4)			45/9=E (4)
75/3=Y (2)	25/5=E (2)	36/3=L (2)	56/8=G (4)	15/3=E (1)			36/2=R (4)
		15/3=E (4)	40/5=H (2)	39/3=M (1)	5/1=E (4)		
	16/4=D (4)		5/5=A (1)	42/6=G (2)			76/4=S (4)
			100/10=J (1)	24/6=D (3)	42/2=U (2)		
	14/2=G (3)	45/3=O (3)	75/5=O (3)		32/4=H (2)		

		39/3=M (4)	4/4=A (4)				46/2=W (4)
	57/3=S (4)			63/7=I (4)	48/4=L (4)		72/8=I (4)
			36/2=R (1)				144/12=L (4)
		38/2=S (1)		25/5=E (1)	100/4=Y (1)		
14/14=A (2)	100/5=T (2)	60/3=T (2)	45/3=O (2)	63/9=G (3)	56/8=G (3)	26/2=M (1)	
			72/8=I (2)		45/3=O (3)		
		36/3=L (2)			12/3=D (3)		

12/6=B (3)					76/4=S (1)	
	36/2=R (3)			13/1=M (1)		
		11/11=A (3)		36/4=I (1)		
	50/5=J (2)		28/2=N (3)		60/3=T (1)	88/8=K (4)
		45/3=O (2)		12/3=D (3)	32/4=H (1)	54/3=R (4)
	52/2=Z (4)	42/3=N (2)	81/9=I (4)	44/2=V (4)	12/12=A (4)	
		20/1=T (4)	15/3=E (2)	57/3=S (2)		

PAGE 96

		46/2=W (4)	14/14=A (4)	48/4=L (4)		6/6=A (4)
					60/5=L (4)	9/3=C (4)
		46/2=W (1)	63/7=I (1)	50/2=Y (2)		15/3=E (4)
40/5=H (1)	25/5=E (1)		32/8=D (2)	100/5=T (1)	60/3=T (1)	
			34/34=A (2)			28/2=N (3)
		16/8=B (2)	54/3=R (2)	42/3=N (3)		45/3=O (3)
	18/6=C (3)	144/12=L (3)	72/8=I (3)		40/2=T (3)	

76/4=S (4)						
	39/3=M (4)	19/1=S (2)		15/3=E (1)		
12/12=A (4)			35/7=E (2)	48/4=L (1)	75/3=Y (3)	
	144/12=L (4)		15/15=A (1)	42/3=N (2)		55/11=E (3)
60/5=L (4)		40/5=H (1)			45/3=O (2)	54/3=R (3)
46/2=W (4)	45/3=O (4)	18/6=C (1)			50/5=J (2)	36/2=R (3)
	26/2=M (1)	75/5=O (4)	12/3=D (4)	21/7=C (3)	4/4=A (3)	

			15/15=A (1)	42/3=N (1)		18/3=F (4)
		32/4=H (1)				72/8=I (4)
15/3=E (2)			40/2=T (1)		28/2=N (3)	76/4=S (4)
	6/2=C (2)	42/3=N (4)	14/14=A (1)	42/2=U (4)	30/6=E (3)	40/5=H (4)
	35/7=E (4)	11/11=A (2)	36/2=R (4)	36/3=L (1)	10/5=B (4)	84/7=L (3)
		54/3=R (2)				60/5=L (3)
			56/8=G (2)		15/15=A (3)	

	√49=G (4)	√64=H (3)	√81=I (3)	√196=N (3)		
√196=N (4)	√361=S (3)		√49=G (3)	√225=O (1)		
√81=I (4)	√1=A (3)		√4=B (1)	√400=T (3)	√196=N (1)	
√16=D (4)	√529=W (3)			√225=O (3)	√16=D (1)	
√225=O (4)			√196=N (3)		√400=T (2)	√361=S (1)
	√225=O (4)	√256=P (2)			√400=T (2)	
	√49=G (4)		√324=R (2)	√1=A (2)		

						√225=O (4)
		√121=K (1)	√196=N (2)		√361=S (4)	√196=N (4)
			√9=C (1)	√25=E (2)	√324=R (4)	
	√196=N (3)	√25=E (3)	√225=O (1)	√25=E (2)		√25=E (4)
		√324=R (1)	√256=P (3)		√64=H (2)	√16=D (4)
		√256=P (3)			√361=S (2)	√196=N (4)
√256=P (3)	√81=I (3)				√1=A (4)	

√169=M (4)	√9=C (4)	√16=D (4)	√225=O (4)	√196=N (4)	√25=E (3)	
		√81=I (1)	√196=N (1)	√144=L (3)	√1=A (4)	
	√529=W (1)	√144=L (2)	√16=D (3)	√361=S (1)		√144=L (4)
		√144=L (2)	√1=A (3)	√144=L (1)	√16=D (4)	√400=T (1)
	√81=I (2)		√25=E (3)		√25=E (1)	
		√64=H (2)		√64=H (3)		
				√9=C (3)		

	√100=J (2)	√225=O (2)				√49=G (4)
	√196=N (2)				√1=A (4)	
	√25=E (2)		√81=I (1)	√400=T (1)	√361=S (4)	
√361=S (2)		√169=M (1)			√400=T (4)	√64=H (3)
		√169=M (1)		√441=U (4)	√81=I (3)	√81=I (4)
			√441=U (1)	√1=A (4)	√144=L (3)	√196=N (4)
			√361=S (1)		√25=E (4)	√144=L (3)

		√1=A (3)	√324=R (3)			
	√49=G (3)		√196=N (3)	√81=I (1)	√169=M (1)	
		√25=E (3)	√144=L (1)			√400=T (4)
			√324=R (3)	√144=L (1)		√81=I (4)
√25=E (4)	√4=B (2)		√324=R (1)	√25=E (1)	√169=M (4)	
√121=K (4)		√144=L (2)	√441=U (2)	√25=E (4)	√4=B (4)	
	√1=A (4)	√144=L (4)	√324=R (4)	√196=N (2)	√400=T (2)	

√81=I (1)	√144=L (1)				√25=E (2)	√361=S (2)
√1=A (1)		√144=L (1)			√196=N (2)	
	√169=M (1)	√81=I (1)				√225=O (2)
	√361=S (1)	√25=E (3)	√529=W (1)		√100=J (2)	
	√324=R (3)	√400=T (3)	√324=R (3)		√529=W (4)	√225=O (4)
			√1=A (3)	√400=T (4)	√225=O (4)	
	√25=E (4)	√1=A (4)	√361=S (4)	√9=C (3)		√16=D (4)

PAGE 105

		√169=M (3)	√361=S (3)			
		√1=A (3)	√64=H (2)			√400=T (1)
√196=N (2)		√25=E (2)	√16=D (3)		√324=R (1)	
	√225=O (2)	√196=N (2)	√1=A (3)	√441=U (1)		
√121=K (4)	√361=S (2)	√81=I (4)	√9=C (3)	√169=M (1)		
	√9=C (4)	√169=M (3)	√16=D (4)		√256=P (1)	
	√324=R (4)	√225=O (4)	√16=D (4)			

PAGE 106

	√4=B (3)			√16=D (4)		√529=W (1)
	√81=I (3)		√25=E (1)		√25=E (4)	√64=H (1)
√25=E (3)		√169=M (2)		√400=T (1)	√81=I (1)	√9=C (4)
√4=B (3)		√225=O (2)				√1=A (4)
	√25=E (3)		√225=O (2)	√324=R (2)		√256=P (4)
	√324=R (3)			√25=E (2)	√324=R (4)	
				√225=O (4)	√81=I (4)	

PAGE 107

	$\sqrt{400}$=T (1)				$\sqrt{49}$=G (3)	
$\sqrt{64}$=H (1)		$\sqrt{81}$=I (1)	$\sqrt{169}$=M (1)	$\sqrt{81}$=I (3)	$\sqrt{121}$=K (4)	$\sqrt{196}$=N (3)
			$\sqrt{324}$=R (3)	$\sqrt{361}$=S (1)	$\sqrt{9}$=C (4)	$\sqrt{225}$=O (3)
		$\sqrt{324}$=R (3)			$\sqrt{225}$=O (4)	
	$\sqrt{25}$=E (3)	$\sqrt{144}$=L (2)	$\sqrt{25}$=E (2)	$\sqrt{9}$=C (4)		
	$\sqrt{36}$=F (3)		$\sqrt{196}$=N (4)	$\sqrt{529}$=W (2)	$\sqrt{81}$=I (2)	
		$\sqrt{1}$=A (4)	$\sqrt{64}$=H (4)		$\sqrt{361}$=S (2)	

PAGE 108

$\sqrt{144}$=L (1)						
	$\sqrt{225}$=O (1)		$\sqrt{361}$=S (1)		$\sqrt{144}$=L (3)	$\sqrt{1}$=A (3)
	$\sqrt{256}$=P (1)	$\sqrt{25}$=E (1)		$\sqrt{225}$=O (3)		
	$\sqrt{25}$=E (4)		$\sqrt{196}$=N (3)		$\sqrt{4}$=B (2)	
$\sqrt{361}$=S (4)	$\sqrt{64}$=H (4)	$\sqrt{361}$=S (3)	$\sqrt{400}$=T (4)	$\sqrt{441}$=U (2)		
$\sqrt{400}$=T (4)	$\sqrt{9}$=C (4)	$\sqrt{441}$=U (4)	$\sqrt{225}$=O (3)	$\sqrt{361}$=S (2)		
	$\sqrt{196}$=N (4)		$\sqrt{64}$=H (2)			

			√196=N (2)	√196=N (2)	√225=O (2)	
	√256=P (4)	√225=O (4)	√25=E (2)	√1=A (4)		√196=N (2)
√1=A (4)		√144=L (2)	√484=V (4)		√25=E (1)	√400=T (3)
	√324=R (4)			√196=N (3)	√144=L (1)	√400=T (3)
		√1=A (4)	√324=R (3)	√225=O (1)	√25=E (3)	
	√49=G (3)	√1=A (3)	√64=H (4)	√9=C (1)		
			√361=S (4)			

		√4=B (2)		√1=A (4)	√400=T (4)	
		√1=A (2)	√144=L (2)	√25=E (4)	√36=F (1)	√64=H (4)
	√9=C (2)	√225=O (1)	√529=W (4)		√324=R (1)	√25=E (4)
√121=K (2)		√625=Y (4)	√9=C (1)	√1=A (1)		√324=R (4)
	√1=A (4)			√196=N (1)		√400=T (3)
√169=M (4)	√256=P (3)	√81=I (3)			√400=T (3)	
		√196=N (3)	√121=K (3)	√25=E (3)		

			√196=N (3)			
	√196=N (2)	√225=O (3)	√361=S (3)	√324=R (2)	√1=A (2)	√169=M (2)
		√81=I (2)	√400=T (2)	√4=B (3)		
√16=D (4)				√25=E (1)	√81=I (3)	
	√324=R (4)		√361=S (1)	√169=M (1)	√64=H (4)	√49=G (3)
	√25=E (4)			√25=E (4)	√81=I (1)	√361=S (4)
		√64=H (4)	√256=P (4)		√324=R (1)	

	√144=L (4)	√16=D (4)	√361=S (1)			
√400=T (4)	√169=M (3)	√1=A (4)		√169=M (1)		
√225=O (4)		√81=I (3)	√144=L (3)	√81=I (1)		√324=R (3)
	√196=N (4)		√400=T (1)	√144=L (3)	√25=E (3)	
	√49=G (2)			√64=H (1)		
		√441=U (2)	√25=E (2)			√1=A (2)
				√400=T (2)	√400=T (2)	

			√25=E (4)	√324=R (4)			
	√81=I (3)	√169=M (4)					
	√169=M (4)	√361=S (3)	√324=R (1)	√25=E (1)			
√81=I (4)	√529=W (4)	√225=O (1)	√361=S (3)			√324=R (2)	√16=D (2)
	√64=H (4)	√225=O (1)	√1=A (3)	√81=I (2)			
	√169=M (1)	√9=C (4)	√49=G (3)	√4=B (2)			
		√361=S (4)	√1=A (3)				

		√324=R (1)	√400=T (1)				
	√225=O (1)	√361=S (3)	√144=L (1)	√196=N (3)			√144=L (2)
	√196=N (3)	√529=W (1)	√225=O (3)	√1=A (1)			√25=E (2)
	√64=H (3)		√81=I (4)	√256=P (1)	√361=S (2)		
√100=J (3)	√225=O (3)		√361=S (4)	√9=C (4)	√144=L (2)		
			√25=E (2)	√81=I (2)	√196=N (4)		
		√36=F (4)	√324=R (4)	√1=A (4)			

√225=O (1)	√529=W (1)						
√225=O (1)	√324=R (1)	√169=M (4)				√361=S (2)	
√16=D (1)	√361=S (4)	√225=O (1)	√1=A (4)			√256=P (2)	√25=E (2)
		√196=N (1)	√81=I (4)	√169=M (2)			√625=Y (2)
			√144=L (4)	√25=E (2)	√144=L (3)		
		√144=L (4)	√16=D (2)		√144=L (3)	√25=E (3)	
		√529=W (4)	√81=I (4)		√1=A (3)	√196=N (3)	

			√16=D (3)	√324=R (3)			
				√196=N (2)	√225=O (3)		
√64=H (1)	√81=I (1)	√225=O (4)	√1=A (2)		√36=F (3)		
	√196=N (4)	√144=L (1)	√64=H (4)	√16=D (2)			√121=K (3)
√625=Y (4)		√144=L (1)	√324=R (2)	√400=T (4)	√9=C (3)		
	√100=J (2)	√225=O (2)	√196=N (4)		√25=E (3)		
			√1=A (4)	√4=B (3)			